Tales from the Table

of related interest

Applied Behaviour Analysis and Autism
Building A Future Together
Edited by Mickey Keenan, Mary Henderson, Ken P. Kerr and Karola Dillenburger
Foreword by Professor Gina Green
ISBN 978 1 84310 310 3

Video Modelling and Behaviour Analysis
A Guide for Teaching Social Skills to Children with Autism
Christos Nikopoulos and Mickey Keenan
Foreword by Sandy Hobbs
ISBN 978 1 84310 338 7

Parents' Education as Autism Therapists
Applied Behaviour Analysis in Context
Edited by Mickey Keenan, Ken P. Kerr and Karola Dillenburger
Foreword by Bobby Newman
ISBN 978 1 85302 778 9

Raising a Child with Autism
A Guide to Applied Behavior Analysis for Parents
Shira Richman
ISBN 978 1 85302 910 3

The Complete Guide to Asperger's Syndrome
Tony Attwood
ISBN 978 1 84310 495 7

Asperger's Syndrome
A Guide for Parents and Professionals
Tony Attwood
Foreword by Lorna Wing
ISBN 978 1 85302 577 8

Tales from the Table

Lovaas/ABA Intervention with Children on the Autistic Spectrum

Margaret Anderson

Jessica Kingsley Publishers
London and Philadelphia

First published in 2007
by Jessica Kingsley Publishers
116 Pentonville Road
London N1 9JB, UK
and
400 Market Street, Suite 400
Philadelphia, PA 19106, USA

www.jkp.com

Library of Congress Cataloging in Publication Data
A CIP catalog record for this book is available from the Library of Congress

British Library Cataloguing in Publication Data
A CIP catalogue record for this book is available from the British Library

ISBN 978 1 84310 306 6

Printed and bound in the United States by Thomson-Shore, Inc.

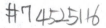

Contents

Chapter 1

Introduction

Since the mid-1990s autism has been a 'hot' topic in the field of education. The inclusion of children on the autistic spectrum in mainstream schools, the challenges faced by students in higher education who have these particular difficulties, what constitutes appropriate early intervention: these are among the issues that present themselves when considering the complex arena that is education for the individual with autistic spectrum disorder. Most of these issues lie outside the remit of this text although they have an influence upon its topic. Most of the material in this book pertains to one topic only – early intensive behavioural intervention.

Aims of the text

In presenting the stories of the five children in this book, I am aiming to 'show not tell': the aim is that the work done with and by the children should demonstrate the utility (or otherwise) of the approach. I hope that the book will give a clear picture of the realities of early intensive behavioural intervention. The first two chapters contextualise the approach; each of the following five chapters tells the story of a young (with one exception) child's learning while following such a programme. The exception is John – he tells his story himself, with a little help from his sister. Each of the stories is told in a straightforward manner, outlining the child's progress over weeks, months and years of intervention. Each chapter also includes a different perspective on involvement with the work, including a parental perspective, a tutor's perspective and the perspective of a teacher from a mainstream school which one of the children attended. In two of the chapters, the child's sibling has written about his or her experience of having a brother undertaking this specialist education. I trust that the immediacy of the narrative will assist the reader in gaining a picture of the realities of running such a programme, as opposed to the theory behind it.

The material is intended as neither an advertisement for nor a testimony against this particular intervention. Real accounts are offered to further our knowledge of what undertaking this education means for individual children, their families and those involved with them. In choosing the five children, I have used what a researcher might call a 'convenience sample': children who are known to me and whose families, tutors and schools were willing to be involved in the project. The children are representative only insofar as that they have had intensive behavioural intervention. I have not chosen 'best-outcome' children, so the tales are not all of children indistinguishable from their typically developing peers. Neither have I chosen those for whom the approach had little impact – to reiterate, this is a convenience sample. I hope that, in telling their stories, I have avoided the worst excesses of the range of autism intervention literature: the dry 'how-to' manual at one end and the 'miracle' revelations at the other.

Thus, this book is potentially helpful to parents considering this intervention for their children, professionals from a variety of backgrounds within the autism education arena who may know little about the approach and professionals who are very familiar with the approach who may be interested in another practitioner's work. I hope also it will be interesting to anyone who wishes to share the joy and celebration of these children's achievements.

Organisation of the book

This book does not offer an academic commentary on the research and debates – political, technical and moral – around early intensive behavioural intervention, as this would not add to the validity of the children's stories. For anyone who is keen to follow up these aspects of the work, the rich and growing literature in the field is readily available in journals and on the internet, and reference will be made to appropriate reading as we progress. However, some issues do need to be addressed if the reader is to understand the context of the stories. Thus, the remainder of this introduction aims to cover the 'essentials' of early intensive behavioural intervention. The first area addressed is that of the relationship between the various, somewhat scary-sounding concepts that litter the literature: applied behavioural analysis; early intensive behavioural intervention; Lovaas. It also gives an account of the historical and current status of these approaches, reflecting on the consequent issues faced by the parents in the book.

Chapter 2 contextualises the intervention within the broader field of special needs education. In order to do this, a broad view is taken of the whole position of autism within the field of cognitive impairment. How and why this intervention (along with other autism early interventions) has become a special case within special needs will be considered. This chapter also considers the state of societal play for individuals with cognitive differences of all kinds and, in light of that discussion, consideration is given to why parents might want to choose this particular early intervention for their child. Chapter 8 opens out the field of thought again and looks toward the future in light of emerging political trends in the world of autism. I trust this part of the book will enable the reader to make links between the intricate, detailed work that forms the basis of the narratives to the wider world of disability politics. The more impatient reader may wish to cut straight to Chapters 3–7, the children's stories. If you do this, please return to these opening chapters, as they provide the background to the perhaps more interesting narrative material.

What are behavioural approaches to autism?

For the parent or professional new to the field of early intervention for the child with autism, the plethora of approaches may seem daunting. This section of our introduction aims to give a simple outline of the field, beginning with how behavioural approaches differ from others.

Psychology is the study of human thought and behaviour. Within the discipline of psychology, many different schools of thought co-exist, each holding different beliefs about the nature of thought and behaviour and consequently recommending different approaches to help those in need. For example, a psychoanalytic approach would suggest that the human personality is formed from structures that, in response to environmental demands, shape our behaviour. Any psychopathology in the individual is addressed through exploration of these structures and their contents through individual psychoanalytic therapy. Behavioural approaches, on the other hand, would suggest that individuals acquire behaviour through interaction with their environments and that we learn behaviours that are helpful to us in any given situation (Atkinson and Hilgard 1996; Myers 2003). Thus, a number of approaches to working with the child with autism spring from these various schools within the discipline. Options (Son-Rise in the US) is based on humanistic psychology; the approach outlined in this text is based on behavioural psychology.

Within the school of behavioural perspectives on teaching, there are a number of different approaches that are often used together, often overlap and are frequently confused. A short explanation of some of the terms that commonly occur in the literature is given below, the purpose being to clarify the approach taken with each of the children in the text.

- *Applied behavioural analysis* – this is the use of the scientific principles of behaviour to form, maintain and increase desired behaviours and to diminish less desirable behaviours. This can involve a number of different strategies and can be used across a wide variety of situations and people in order to change/teach behaviour.

- '*Behaviour analytic treatment* for autism focuses on teaching small, measurable units of behaviour systematically' (Green 1996, p.30, my italics). The important points here are that the steps are small enough for the child to be successful and that we are focusing on behaviour. The focus of the teaching is on the observable – can the child order the numbers one to ten? – rather than our assumptions/best guesses about what he knows. Whilst clearly helpful, this approach as outlined raises the question of which skills to teach and how?

- *The Lovaas programme* – the evolution of early intensive behavioural intervention in the UK (see below) has led to much confusion over what constitutes a Lovaas programme. In order to clarify this issue, I present the elements of best practice taken from current research in the area (Bibby *et al.* 2002; Howard *et al.* 2005; Sallows and Graupner 2005; Smith 1999). A Lovaas programme requires that a discrete trial teaching approach is taken with the child, the Lovaas curriculum should be followed and the teaching should be intensive – ideally 40 hours per week.

To expand on these points: in relation to the use of discrete trial teaching, clearly as the child gains more skills and is able to learn alongside his or her peers, so he or she needs to learn in a more 'typical' fashion. However, at the beginning of the programme, the child is taught using a three-part chain:

the instruction/request → the child's response →   a consequence
                                                    (generally a reward)

This simple chain is used to teach a whole range of knowledge and skills and is an effective way of introducing new information, skills and ideas to any child (Anderson, Taras and O'Malley Cannon 1996). However, as the aim of the programme is to prepare children for schooling alongside typically developing children, the child with autism will need to aquire the ability to learn in the manner adopted in most classrooms. Thus, the later parts of the child's programme will prepare him or her for new teaching/learning approaches (Leaf and McEachin 1999).

The Lovaas curriculum is a fairly standard, although very detailed, developmental curriculum, tackling the areas one would wish to address with all pre-schoolers – communication, self-care skills, knowledge about the world. However, it is specific to the child on the autistic spectrum, as it uses the child's strengths in order to meet his or her needs. It also starts (where needed) from the point of gaining and holding the child's attention and addressing any undesirable behaviours.

The final point of the intensity of the programme is that which causes most debate – how intensive is intensive? This is clearly not just a matter of hours; other factors are also important – how many teaching/learning opportunities are presented in the time available? How reinforcing is the tutor and, therefore, how hard will the child try with him or her? Are the right skills being targeted? However, the research would indicate that children who have been most successful are those who have had at least 30 hours' teaching/learning per week (Green 1996). A related question here and one that is important to parents and the bodies funding the programme is that of duration. A quick review of some of the literature (Anderson *et al.* 1987; Bibby *et al.* 2002; Sheinkopf and Siegel 1998; Smith, Groen and Wynn 2000) demonstrates that two years is about average, and this would fit with the concept of 'early' intervention.

This rather dry material relates directly to the children and families in this book: four of the five programmes of learning described here started with the children being between two and four years old. At the beginning of their programmes, a discrete trial approach was adopted and the Lovaas curriculum followed. Toward the end of the programmes, and as needs change, other approaches from within the ABA (applied behavioural analysis) arena were included in their learning. The other child, John, began work at the age of 11 and so a combination of discrete trial teaching, programmes from the Lovaas curriculum, broader ABA and some cognitive strategies were used in teaching him. Whilst practitioners need to be clear about the approach used with a child, one should always remember that it is the child who is central, not the programme.

Early intensive behavioural intervention in the UK

My experience of working with families in the UK undertaking Lovaas/ABA programmes has been of families not seeking a 'cure' or being unable to accept their child's difficulties, but of parents aiming to do as much as they can to support their child's early development. The vast majority of these families are well read in the field of autism education and have made an informed choice of this approach. Given the intensity of the work which it involves, why would parents opt for this early intensive behavioural intervention?

The National Autistic Society survey (1997) indicates that families are dissatisfied with the support and help they receive from statutory services and that the little help they can gain has to be fought for. While this survey is no longer new, my recent and current experience with families would suggest little improvement in this situation. Families' dissatisfaction runs the whole life span of their offspring with autism, beginning with diagnosis and ending with the search for appropriate residential/supported living accommodation. The issue here is that of early education: while statutory providers differ in the amount and type of in-home support and nursery/pre-school provision offered, parents feel that it is not sufficient to make the most of the developmental opportunities within these first five years of a child's life. Some areas offer in-home teaching (e.g. Portage), while others offer a specialist nursery/pre-school placement. The availability of speech and language therapy varies enormously throughout the country, as does access to appropriate occupational therapy assessment and input. Parents, aware on the one hand of the research on prognosis and on the other of the brevity of the 'early intervention' period, feel that, in order to make the most of their child's development, a more intensive approach is needed (Couper 2004).

During the 1980s and 1990s, when parents began to ask for early behavioural intervention, the resources to provide it did not exist within the UK. Parents were incredibly resourceful and professionals from the US and the Scandinavian countries were contacted and employed to run programmes through workshops every three to four months. Parents took the major responsibility for the running of the programme: they employed tutorial staff, arranged work schedules, kept on top of the paper work, took part in the child's education and liaised with the supervisor, as well as being parents. These families often asked the (then) local education authorities to fund the programmes – this request was often refused and led to an appeal to the Special Educational Needs (now, and Disability) Tribunal.

Throughout the 1990s and the first decade of the twenty-first century, more professionals have become available within the UK to run home education programmes, either through organisations such as Peach (Parents for the Early intervention of Autism) or working independently. University departments are paying more attention to ABA, in terms of both research (the SCAmP project at Southampton) and preparing professionals (for example at the University of Ulster). Unfortunately, little else has changed in the intervening years and the situation described above is one in which families frequently find themselves. Typically, parents continue to shoulder the major workload in running a home programme, even once it is funded by the local authority. Families frequently need to organise and attend a tribunal hearing to gain what they perceive to be an appropriate education for their child.

Thus we currently have a rather unsatisfactory situation in which Lovaas/ABA professionals are unregulated, in which parents take a much greater responsibility for the day-to-day organisation of their child's education than one would typically anticipate. Further, the more optimistic professionals of the 1990s anticipated that this type of intervention might become part of the range of services offered by statutory providers of education, given that it has (at the very least) comparable research support to more commonly used approaches. However, this has not evolved, and parents wishing to undertake this work with their child continue to face a struggle in order to do so. In working with parents on this book, the issue of the wrangling they felt took place with education authorities was quite prominent in their thoughts and recollections and I have tried to reflect the additional strain this caused in the text.

The organisation of the programmes

Two of the five programmes described were run on a workshop basis. That is, following screening (for suitability) and pre-intervention testing (of cognitive, language and social performance) I visited the family home for a two-day start-up workshop. The tutors, who were recruited by the family, implemented the programme as instructed, with frequent communication with me between workshops. Thereafter, I visited the child and team at home every six to eight weeks, evaluating the child's learning, checking for consistency in teaching across team members, moving the programme along and liaising with education and other service providers (e.g. speech and language therapists) involved with the children. The other programmes were run on the basis of a visit every two to four weeks; one was run by another supervisor with overview from me.

The tutorial staff employed to work with the children described came from a wide range of backgrounds. Many were under- and post-graduate psychology or education students, who have gone on to work in other fields with children with special needs. I have learned a lot from them and am grateful for the hard work they undertook.

Ending programmes is often difficult – enabling all involved to step back from the intensity and focus of the programme is challenging, but necessary for a smooth transition to school and, again, I hope this is reflected in the text.

I am honoured that the children and families felt able to share their stories with me and thus with you. I hope these accounts will enable you to move away from the dogma that too often plagues discussions in the field and open the way for the broader thinking suggested in the final chapter. Please enjoy hearing these tales, as I have enjoyed these children.

References

Anderson, S., Avery, D., DiPietro, E. Edwards, G. and Christian, W. (1987) 'Intensive home-based intervention with autistic children.' *Education and Treatment of Children*, 10, 352–66.

Anderson, S., Taras, M. and O'Malley Cannon, B. (1996) 'Teaching new skills to young children with autism.' In C. Maurice, G. Green and S. Luce (eds) *Behavioural Intervention for Young Children with Autism*. Austin, TX: Pro-Ed.

Atkinson, R. and Hilgard, E. (1996) *Hilgard's Introduction to Psychology*. London: Harcourt.

Bibby, P., Eikeseth, S., Martin, N., Mudford, O. and Reeves, D. (2002) 'Progress and outcomes for children with autism receiving parent-managed intensive interventions.' *Research in Developmental Disabilities*, 23, 81–104.

Couper, J. (2004) 'Who should pay for intensive behavioural intervention in autism? A parent's view.' *Journal of Paediatrics and Child Health*, 40 (9–10), 559–61.

Green, G. (1996) 'Early behavioural intervention for autism – What does the research tell us?' In C. Maurice, G. Green and S. Luce (eds) *Behavioural Intervention for Young Children with Autism*. Austin, TX: Pro-Ed.

Howard, J., Sparkman, C., Cohen, H., Green, G. and Stanislaw, H. (2005) 'A comparison of intensive behavioural analytic and eclectic treatments for young children with autism.' *Research in Developmental Disabilities*, 26, 359–83.

Leaf, R. and McEachin, J. (1999) *A Work in Progress – Behaviour Management Strategies and a Curriculum for Intensive Behavioural Treatment of Autism*. New York: DRL Books.

Myers, D. (2003) *Psychology*. New York: Worth Publishers.

National Autistic Society (1997) *Beyond Rain Man – Experiences of and Attitudes Toward Autism*. London: National Autistic Society.

Sallows, G. and Graupner, T. (2005) 'Intensive behavioural treatment for children with autism: Four-year outcomes and predictors.' *American Journal on Mental Retardation*, 110 (6), 417–38.

Sheinkopf, S. and Siegel, B. (1998) 'Home-based behavioural treatment of young children with autism.' *Journal of Autism and Developmental Disorders*, 28, 15–23.

Smith, T. (1999) 'Outcome of early intervention for children with autism.' *Clinical Psychology: Science and Practice*, 6, 33–49.

Smith, T., Groen, A. and Wynn, J. (2000) 'Randomised trial of intensive early intervention for children with pervasive developmental disorder.' *American Journal on Mental Retardation*, 105, 269–85.

Further reading

On the psychology and ABA 'basics'

Glassman, W. (2000) *Approaches in Psychology*. Buckingham: Open University Press.

This is a sound introductory text that outlines different approaches clearly.

Myers, D. (2003) *Psychology*. New York: Worth Publishers.

This is a huge introductory textbook, but has excellent stand-alone chapters on different approaches within psychology.

On 'Lovaas' research

Bibby, P., Eikeseth, S., Martin, N., Mudford, O. and Reeves, D. (2002) 'Progress and outcomes for children with autism receiving parent-managed intensive interventions.' *Research in Developmental Disabilities*, 23, 81–104.

Green, G. (1996) 'Early behavioural intervention for autism – What does the research tell us?' In C. Maurice, G. Green and S. Luce (eds) *Behavioural Intervention for Young Children with Autism*. Austin, TX: Pro-Ed.

Howard, J., Sparkman, C., Cohen, H., Green, G. and Stanislaw, H. (2005) 'A comparison of intensive behavioural analytic and eclectic treatments for young children with autism.' *Research in Developmental Disabilities*, 26, 359–83.

Sallows, G. and Graupner, T. (2005) 'Intensive behavioural treatment for children with autism: Four-year outcomes and predictors.' *American Journal on Mental Retardation*, 110 (6), 417–38.

On running a programme

See the PEACH website at www.peach.org.uk/ManagingaProgramme

Independent autism practitioner

Margaret Anderson

Tel: (+44) 01255 678 493 or 0777 550 8651

Email: Dr.Mags@fredrick499.fsnet.co.uk

Chapter 2

Contextualising Autism and Early Intensive Behavioural Intervention

Autism has become rather a fashionable topic – much more so than the range of other cognitive difficulties that can delay/disorder a child's development or hinder an adult's functioning. As such, it tends to be viewed in isolation and much of the commonality that children and adults with autistic spectrum disorder share with people with other cognitive deficits tends to be over-looked.

Autism as disability?

Whilst some might argue (see Baron-Cohen 2004) that the absence of additional learning difficulties removes the person with autism from the 'disability' range, the difficulties in accessing and accomplishing ordinary life experiences faced by this group would militate against this position. The rates of un- or underemployment (Walker-Sperry 2001), difficulties with relation-ships of all kinds (Slater-Walker and Slater-Walker 2002), levels of mental and emotional dis-ease (Morgan 1996) surely tell us something about the effect of cognitive difference/disability on the person's ability to function effectively and happily. The approach which advocates that we differentiate people with 'just' autism from those with an additional learning difficulty seems to me to be taking the first steps on a path littered with difficulties – of a moral, political and practical nature.

To address the least important of these first: how can we differentiate with any degree of reliability those with or without learning difficulties additional to their autism? The types of assessments used to gauge intelligence will give a 'ball park' number at the end but tell us little about how the individual's skills or needs scatter affects their ability to learn skills that will be useful to them. For example, I have worked with some children with very high IQ scores who found mastering simple self-care skills extremely challenging and who thus might present as children with global delay. When assessing adults, this differentiation of the difficulties caused by any additional learning disability and those caused by the individual's autism become even more hazy as one is trying to see through what Valerie Sinason (1992) calls the 'secondary handicaps' – the means through which the individual has learned to deal with the world.

From a political perspective, this differentiation of those with from those without additional cognitive issues would seem to be unhelpful. Many of the aims of advocacy groups for people with learning disabilities are congruent with those of adults with autism: a society more open to differences, legislation to protect and enhance legal and civil rights, appropriate and sufficiently funded support and so on (see Ramcharan *et al.* 1997). That each minority group should tackle these issues separately would appear to be a waste of effort where a cohesive political movement for those with cognitive differences may have more chance of success.

Finally, I think there is a moral issue here: above we have touched upon the discrimination experienced by people with learning disabilities in everyday life. To differentiate those people who, by reason of additional learning disabilities, are not part of the 'autism movement' is a further reinforcement of the very attitudes one would wish to dismantle. Of course, the presence of additional learning needs means that some people may experience life very differently from others. But if there is one thing that comes over very clearly from all of the literature in the field of autism, it is that very divergence of experience, even among those who are 'just autistic'.

The social view of disability

Thus, if we can place autism within the wider disability spectrum, we can reflect the range of opinions around the broader topic onto the narrower and perhaps the first of these should be the question of the validity of any intervention at all for people with autism or, indeed, any other cognitive delay/difference. Oliver (1990) suggests that we can view disability as socially constructed: thus the exclusion and prejudice that are faced by people with difficulties are not facets of their 'condition'; rather, they reflect a lack of societal accommodation and understanding. This is the obverse of the more prevalent medical model that places the deficit squarely within the individual. Thus, in applying the societal debate to people with autism, we might argue that a culture more tolerant of difference and less intent on having everyone behave in the same manner might not see autism as a disability.

Whilst undoubtedly people with any form of disability face obstacles to functioning within a culture that is not geared to providing access, employment and so on to people with difficulties, this approach has detractors even within the disability world. Thomas (1999) suggests that to ignore the 'impairment' aspect of a person's condition is to belittle the very real difficulties raised by the person's condition – for example, lack of mobility or low vision. In relation to autistic spectrum disorder, to suggest that if organisations and individuals were more tolerant then the autistic person would necessarily be happier or more fulfilled reflects a lack of understanding of the condition. While undoubtedly attitudes to people with any type of difference need to be more tolerant, merely changing environments, attitudes and practices will not solve the enormous challenges faced on a daily basis by people with autism. For example, one chat room recently hosted a discussion on the problems of forgetting to eat, the undesirable physical effects of this and the various strategies individuals had developed to overcome this problem. A change in societal attitude would not enable an individual to read bodily signals more acutely. Similarly, abolishing homework would relieve some pressure on many young people with autistic spectrum disorder (and their families) but would not address the underlying issue – that the nature of autistic spectrum disorder calls for such intense work through the course of the day that further demands are just too much. While I am not suggesting that changes to societal structures and processes would not be helpful, I do suggest that, when taken alone, this approach overlooks some fundamentals about autism or, indeed, other cognitive difficulties (Gillberg 2002).

In the final chapter of the text, we consider the position of autism advocates – that is, adults with autism who feel that the type of intervention described in this text is, in reality, an attack upon the nature of an individual and thus an assault on their human rights. This group is vociferous in demands for autism to be recognised as just a difference. For example, Jim Sinclair (1993) asks that parents of children with autism should not 'push for the things your expectations tell you are normal' but should accept the autistic child as she or he is. This is a seductive approach which harmonises well with our liberal desire to respect the individual and his or her rights. However, it is important to remember that all parents are engaged in the process of 'gently draw[ing] their beloved baby into a relationship with the world' (Dowty and Colinshaw 2001, p.11) and this entails enabling the child to function optimally within his or her environment. One path that parents might choose to take in order to facilitate this learning for their child is early intensive behavioural intervention. Similarly, as adults, we continue to learn and to adapt to new demands, whatever our start point. In summary: societal change and accommodation is vital to address the discrimination faced by all people with differences; learning about living successfully in the world is vital for all of us.

Setting the scene
Changing policy
The world of learning disability has changed enormously over the past 30 years and early intervention (medical, educational, familial) has played a major part in this change. Changes in any social arena do not occur within a cultural vacuum and we must look to the concurrent political, economic and moral climate to trace the rationale for changes in the lives of people with all types of learning disabilities.

By the middle of the twentieth century, the outcomes of the Wood Report (1929), which established the need for community and residential care for the client group, had become reality and a large number of institutions for people with learning disabilities existed in the UK. Formerly colonies, these became hospitals under the 1946 NHS Act and continued to provide a 'home' to large numbers of people through to the latter part of the century. Classifications of learning disability have changed over the decades (see Atherton 2003) and we have also seen a change in what might be considered a learning disability during this period. Formerly, very able people might have been admitted to an institution for family reasons (Gray and Ridden 1999). Medical science was such that many children with profound learning disabilities and complex health needs did not survive. Thus, there has been a shift in this population through the latter part of the century. However, people with autism have always featured as part of this group. Despite the widening of the diagnostic criteria to include children who at one time might not have attracted a diagnosis, those with autism have always formed part of the 'hospital' population.

Goffman (1961) has described accurately the lifestyle of people who lived in these hospitals. People were not treated as individuals – indeed were 'cared for' in groups. The organisation and processes within the living/working/ leisure environment were geared to ensure that the system worked rather than to meet individual needs. This led, inevitably, to a high degree of depersonalisation. People grew up, lived, worked, socialised and died in isolated (certainly socially, if not geographically) communities, having little contact with more usual lifestyles. These people are beginning to find a voice and a humbling literature is emerging in the field (see Atkinson 1993; Atkinson, Jackson and Walmsley 1997; Atkinson and Williams 1990).

This context is pertinent to our study as many children with autism grew up within these institutions. Whilst the push for de-institutionalisation targeted children as a priority (DOH 1989; Jay Committee 1979), large hospitals continued to have children's wards through the 1970s and 1980s. Indeed, I worked in a large children's ward in the 1970s which provided a home for about 60 children in all, a proportion of whom had autism.

The change in philosophy since then has reflected a societal shift to greater emphasis on individual fulfilment, rights and responsibilities. Thus, as an example, in terms of residential service provision, these years witnessed a move away from large state-run hospitals to smaller community-based private homes. The philosophy underpinning these changes was initially that of normalisation (Whitehead 1992); later, of social role valorisation and, most recently, of inclusion. The emphasis is on the facilitation of ordinary life experiences for the person with disabilities and the right to the opportunities and support the rest of us take for granted.

Atherton (2003) reflects that whilst the shape and constitution of services has altered radically, 'the rate and progress toward helping people with learning disabilities attain socially valued lifestyles have been significantly slower' (p.56). So in this decade we have theoretically a situation in which people with learning disabilities have equal opportunities and inclusion in education, housing and employment, and yet individuals' experiences (see DOH 2001) do not reflect this. Indeed, chat lines for people with autistic spectrum disorder reflect a high degree of exclusion, frustration and isolation despite stated inclusive policies.

Changing education

To return to the children's ward of my past: all of the children attended school, as this was the latter half of the 1970s and the recent Education Act had deemed all children educable. However, the school was in the hospital grounds and catered for all of the children from the hospital plus a few children with disabilities who lived locally. Echoing the changes witnessed in policy for adults, changes in what may be considered to be appropriate education for children with special educational needs have altered the educational landscape hugely. In the UK, a number of Education Acts, most notably the Warnock Report (Warnock 1978) and subsequent Education Act, have emphasised the right of children to de-segregated education and to having their needs met within the mainstream environment. Many children, particularly those with profound difficulties, continue to have their education provided in specialist settings, and the debate continues over whether the mainstream educational environment can adequately meet their needs (Jupp 1992).

Early intervention

The notion of waiting until a child is of school age before addressing his or her educational needs is clearly a nonsense to the vast majority of parents. From birth, we teach our children to relate appropriately to others, to communicate, to play, some self-care skills, to behave appropriately, to care for others and so on. Some parents even tackle literacy and numeracy issues with their children prior to school, but the major part of the young child's education is learning in the realm of socialisation (Burke and Cigno 2000). By definition, some aspects of this learning present more difficulties to the child with cognitive difference than to the typically developing child: which aspects and how much difficulty depends on the environment within which the child finds him- or herself and the expectation therein. Children need to acquire a dazzling breadth and depth of skills and abilities during these early years. Parents of children with special educational needs are very aware of the brevity of this window of opportunity for their children and the need to act quickly to optimise learning during this precious formative period.

Thus, the received wisdom is 'early intervention' for all types of learning disability (Rimland 1998). Parental accounts of statutory services' response to their child's needs make depressing reading (Dowty and Colinshaw 2001; Ives and Munro 2002) and many parents look beyond statutory provision for appropriate intervention. This is particularly so for children with autism, as the research indicates that their cognitive challenges are more amenable than others to early intervention. Whilst the parent of the child with, for example, Down's syndrome may see great steps forward for their child in these early years (Pueschel 2000), the level of improvement in functioning seen in the autistic child undertaking ABA is not likely to be seen in the child with

Down's syndrome. It is this knowledge that so much can be achieved with the child on the autistic spectrum during these formative years that makes the individual case so urgent, and the broader question of appropriate intervention so important.

The range of these debates falls outside the remit of this book. I am, however, constantly amazed that parents who are, at the very least, stressed if not in crisis can access and analyse the vast amount of information available in making decisions on early intervention. As one parent said, 'Autism is what you do for a living; it's our life.' This leads us to the question of why the parents in this book, and many more, decided on the Lovaas approach to early intervention.

Why early intensive behavioural intervention?

In response to the 'Why early intensive behavioural intervention?' question, I merely relate the reasons given by the parents who have contributed to this text. The first of these is that the approach makes sense. In any situation where we are acquiring a skill which is, from the learner's perspective, complex, the teacher will break that skill down into steps that are more easily mastered by the student. This is just what the Lovaas programme does in regard to early skills of attention, co-operation, communication, play, socialisation for children on the autistic spectrum (Maurice 1996). The curriculum teaches areas that are (by diagnostic definition) difficult for the child through the use of areas of strength – an idea not unique to this programme. This simple idea underpins a vast undertaking, as the chapters in this book reveal. Each education team moves with the child, step by step, through an enormous range of skills and abilities along a pre-school curriculum. Much that is covertly learned by typically developing children needs to be overtly taught to the child with autistic spectrum disorder – hence the huge scope of the child's programme.

The second reason often given by parents for choosing this approach is the body of research on which it is based. As above, this text is not concerned with those debates and readers who are interested are directed to the reading indicated in the previous chapter.

The other major reason given by parents for choosing this approach is the level of parental involvement that is crucial to its success (Leaf and McEachin 1999). Whilst not wishing to lend weight to the 'personal tragedy' view of disability (Hevey 1993) many parents' responses to a diagnosis of autism reflect feelings of despair, helplessness and disempowerment (Tommasone and Tommasone 2000). The early intensive behavioural intervention enables parents to engage directly with their child and his or her needs and strengths, working constructively to ameliorate the effects of the condition. By the time parents begin a programme, they are aware of the enormity of the undertaking and appreciate that this is not an approach that can succeed without their commitment. I hope that the enormous efforts made by the parents of the children are reflected in the text. Working with each of the parents has been a humbling and enriching experience for me. I am grateful for the opportunity to have shared in this work and to be able to share that work with others through this book.

References

Atherton, H. (2003) 'A history of learning disabilities.' In B. Gates (ed.) *Learning Disabilities: Toward Inclusion.* Edinburgh: Elsevier Science.

Atkinson, D. (ed.) (1993) *Past Times – Older People with Learning Disabilities Look Back on Their Lives.* Buckingham: Open University Press.

Atkinson, D., Jackson, M. and Walmsley, J. (1997) *Forgotten Lives.* Kidderminster: BILD.

Atkinson, D. and Williams, F. (1990) *Know Me as I am.* London: Hodder and Stoughton.

Baron-Cohen, S. (2004) 'Is Asperger's syndrome/high functioning autism necessarily a disability?' Available at www.geocities.com/CapitolHill/7138lobby/disability.htm (accessed 8 December 2006).

Burke, P. and Cigno, K. (2000) *Learning Disabilities in Children.* Oxford: Blackwell Science.

DOH (1989) *Caring For People: Community Care in the Next Decade and Beyond.* London: HMSO.

DOH (2001) *Valuing People: A New Strategy for Learning Disability in the 21st Century.* London: HMSO.

Dowty, T. and Colinshaw, K. (2001) *Home Educating our Autistic Spectrum Children – Paths are Made by Walking.* London: Jessica Kingsley Publishers.

Gillberg, C. (2002) *A Guide to Asperger Syndrome.* Cambridge: Cambridge University Press.

Goffman, E. (1961) *Asylums: Essays on the Social Situation of Mental Patients and Other Inmates.* Harmondsworth: Penguin.

Gray, B. and Ridden, G. (1999) *Lifemaps of People with Learning Disabilities.* London: Jessica Kingsley Publishers.

Hevey, D. (1993) 'The tragedy principle: Strategies for change in the representation of disabled people.' In J. Swain, S. Finkelstein, S. French and M. Oliver (eds) *Disabling Barriers and Enabling Environments.* London: Sage.

Ives, M. and Munro, N. (2002) *Caring for a Child with Autism: A Practical Guide for Parents.* London: Jessica Kingsley Publishers.

Jay Committee (1979) *Report of the Committee of Enquiry into Mental Handicap Nursing and Care.* London: HMSO.

Jupp, K. (1992) *Everyone Belongs: Inclusive Education for Children with Severe and Profound Learning Disabilities*. London: Souvenir Press.

Leaf, R. and McEachin, J. (eds) (1999) *A Work in Progress – Behavioural Management Strategies and a Curriculum for Intensive Behavioural Treatment of Autism*. New York: DRL Books.

Maurice, C. (ed.) (1996) *Behavioural Intervention for Young Children with Autism*. Austin, TX: Pro-Ed.

Morgan, H. (1996) *Adults with Autism – A Guide to Theory and Practice*. Cambridge: Cambridge University Press.

Oliver, M. (1990) *The Politics of Disablement*. London: Macmillan Press.

Pueschel, S. (2000) *A Patient's Guide to Down Syndrome: Towards a Brighter Future*. Baltimore, MD: Brookes.

Ramcharan, P., Roberts, G., Grant, G. and Borland, J. (eds) (1997) *Empowerment in Everyday Life*. London: Jessica Kingsley Publishers.

Rimland, B. (1998) 'Home programmes evaluated.' *Autism Research Review International*, 12, 2.

Sinason, V. (1992) *Mental Handicap and the Human Condition*. London: Tavistock.

Sinclair, J. (1993) 'Don't mourn for us.' *Autism Network International*, 1, 3. Available at http://web.syr.edu/~jisincla/dontmourn.htm (accessed 8 December 2006).

Slater-Walker, G. and Slater-Walker, C. (2002) *An Asperger Marriage*. London: Jessica Kingsley Publishers.

Thomas, S. (1999) *Female Forms: Experiencing and Understanding Disability*. Buckingham: Open University Press.

Tommasone, L. and Tommasone, J. (2000) 'Adjusting to your child's diagnosis.' In M. Powers (ed.) *Children with Autism – A Parents' Guide*. Rockville, MD: Woodbine House.

Walker-Sperry, V. (2001) *Fragile Success – Ten Autistic Children, Childhood to Adulthood*. Baltimore, MD: Paul Brookes.

Warnock, M. (1978) *Special Educational Needs*. London: HMSO.

Whitehead, S. (1992) 'The social origins of normalisation.' In H. Brown and H. Smith (eds) *Normalisation: A Reader for the 90s*. London: Routledge.

Chapter 3

Sam's Tale

I Can Try

Of all the children whose stories appear in this book, Sam is the easiest to describe. He is an engaging and charming boy of ten years old, who is bright, funny and extraordinarily good company. He is always interesting, always has a contribution to make to a conversation and always makes me laugh. In short, he is a delight.

Sam lives in Surrey with his twin brother Robert, his parents, Alice and Ben, and the family dog. He attends the local junior school on a full-time basis and is due to transfer at the end of the academic year to the senior school. Through his childhood, Sam has had many of the same interests as other boys – dinosaurs, science, football – and his current interest is history. As this chapter reveals, like many people with autistic spectrum disorder who function well in society (see Hadcroft 2004; Williams 1992), Sam is presented by his autism with tremendous challenges that he must face each day to cope with the demands of daily life.

Very early development

Sam had a pretty shaky start in life. He was rather small when born and appeared to have some breathing difficulties which meant he needed to be on a ventilator. Sam was also diagnosed with a diaphragmatic hernia, which led to a nightmare of admission to three different hospitals before surgery was actually undertaken at Great Ormond Street when Sam was aged ten weeks. In the mean time, Sam had had a variety of treatment and investigations for his breathing difficulties and had contracted a hospital-acquired infection. Having been born on 17 February, Sam eventually came home on 1 May.

Sam's health problems continued. He had a hole in his heart which was repaired when he was about one year old and later still (at the age of about two and a half), Sam had his mobile breastbone stabilised. Thus, much of his early life was spent in or around hospitals and receiving medical intervention in one form or another.

As a result, when Sam's parents became concerned about his behaviour as a toddler, myriad causes for unusual development presented themselves: being one of twins; having spent time in hospital; having missed early opportunities for bonding with other family members; having experienced pain and discomfort so young... However, whatever the explanation, Alice and Ben appreciated from early on in Sam's life that he was not developing in the same way as his brother and that he had difficulties with everyday relationships.

Alice and Ben have kept a hugely detailed record of the boys' development and, from this, we were able to trace the course of their concerns for Sam. Alice is also able to remember her emotions very clearly in combination with these notes and mementoes and this has given a very clear picture of the emergence of Sam's difficulties to diagnosis.

Sam's speech developed as one would expect and his motor milestones were also achieved at the normal times. However, Ben and Alice were concerned about his behaviour, as no parenting approaches seemed to work with Sam. He did not respond to the usual combination of reward, negotiation and jollying needed to get small children through the daily routine. His mother describes him as 'mystifyingly unco-operative' and she knew that he wasn't responding in a 'normal' fashion to the world around him. He was not interested in other people's wishes or desires and needed to do things his way and in his own time. Any attempt to alter this regime led to awesome tantrums, physical aggression and huge distress for the whole family. At one point, the family felt that the boys might have fallen into a 'good twin/bad twin' pattern and strove to avoid repeating responses that might strengthen this dynamic. Alice is very clear that, had Sam been a first/only child, she would have been 'suicidal' in response to what she perceived as parental failure with Sam. He was reaching all his developmental milestones but did not respond in any expected way to the emotional world around him. Alice reports (see also Fletcher 1999; Overton 2003) that this felt like a huge failure in parenting and that she did not know where to get help with this very specific yet pervasive problem.

In April 1996, when Sam was just over two years old, the first of a long series of referrals began when Alice took Sam to see his GP – Sam appeared to trip over rather more than should be usual when running. However, he had no language, motor or self-care delay. By the following year, it was very clear that

Sam had some serious behavioural issues: he was continuing to tantrum; he could not be taken into shops; he often refused to walk and had to be carried, kicking and screaming. At this point, a pattern that continues to the time of writing began to emerge in relation to Sam's attendance at nursery.

Early education and starting school

By the time he attended nursery school Sam was toilet trained and was bright and chatty with adults. However, some difficulties began to emerge at nursery, presenting in Sam losing his toileting skills. A visit to a psychologist to help with this led Alice to a rather chilling conclusion – that Sam was simply not interested in pleasing his mother or anyone else in his environment. At this point, when Sam was three and a half years old, the suggestion was made that using routine interval training might help Sam rather than the more person-centred approaches Alice had previously tried.

However, toileting aside, Sam appeared to be coping with nursery. He was quiet in this environment and never drew attention to himself. However, the effort needed to 'keep it together' at nursery was huge and the cost was that Sam's behaviour deteriorated further at home. Throughout his childhood, despite the enormous gains Sam has made, this need to 'let off steam' when he gets home continues to be problematic for his parents and brother, as they are on the receiving end of considerable emotional fall-out from this process.

Sam had been having some speech and language therapy for what were considered to be subtle language difficulties and, although this undoubtedly helped with language pragmatics, his behaviour and interaction continued to deteriorate. An extract from a summary report of a course of speech and language therapy at the end of 1997 reads:

> Behaviour: Sam's behaviour has improved although it is still inconsistent in the sessions. He finds table top activities easier and can get over excited with less structured tasks, throwing pictures and objects inappropriately…

And from a report (different source) five months later: 'Sam did not seem to see why he should do as he was told.'

Sam began school at the age of four and a half. Along with the other children, he attended for half days in the first term, attendance being built up slowly. Alice and Ben were dealing with massive tantrums after school each day and it was clear to them that Sam would not manage whole days at school. As the other children attended full time, Sam continued on a part-time basis.

Alice and Ben describe this time as 'Humpty-Dumpty time' – they spent hours each day putting Sam back together after school. However, during the Easter term, Sam suffered what his parents describe as a breakdown: he refused to go to school, refused to communicate and reverted to talking gibberish. An extract from a journal Alice kept shows the extent of the deterioration in Sam's abilities at this time:

> This morning Sam was talking [in] his very distorted way and lots of gibberish phrases. I knew he would be totally useless at school and felt dreadful (for the teachers) to send him. Picked him up at 1 pm… When we arrived home he lay down in the back and in distorted language said he was too tired to walk. So I babied him and carried him in. He wouldn't even sit in my lap for a story…talking gibberish for a long time… Finally – silence. There was a long silence…

Beginning Sam's programme

Ben and Alice were thus faced with a child who could not be educated in school, who was in poor shape emotionally and physically and whose behaviour was making home life stressful for all family members. Clearly, he needed some very specialist intervention. At this point Sam did not have a diagnosis, although Alice and Ben were fairly sure that autism was at the root of the difficulties Sam was encountering. A few years previously, a paediatrician had given Alice Tony Attwood's (1998) book on Asperger syndrome. While it explained Sam's 'Jekyll and Hyde' personalities in and out of nursery, the book pertains to children older than Sam was at that time and thus it was difficult to apply most of the material to him. However, by this stage it was clear that a diagnosis would be needed in order to move forward with a statement of special educational need and so, at his parents' insistence, Sam was diagnosed – incidentally by the same paediatrician who had given Alice the book on Asperger syndrome years previously. The criteria for Asperger syndrome were discussed at this meeting in the summer of 1999 and eventually a diagnosis of 'atypical autism' was felt to best define Sam's difficulties. However, the clinician noted that, 'He [therefore] does not have the full range of criteria needed for a diagnosis of Asperger syndrome although this may change with time.' Sam's condition has indeed changed over time and 'Asperger syndrome' most closely fits as a description of Sam's current strengths and needs.

Alice researched autism, obtaining information from the National Autistic Society, PEACH and Lovaas organisations in the US. The way in which the

Lovaas programme was delivered appeared to be particularly appropriate for Sam: he focused best in a structured learning environment, he loved adult attention and he worked best on a one-to-one basis. The response from the professionals in the UK to the family's request for Lovaas intervention was very negative, and thus began the long struggle to establish and maintain this intervention. Initially, Alice and Ben were told that Sam was 'too bright' to have a statement of special educational need, despite the fact that he was clearly finding school far too challenging.

As with the other children in the book, Sam's parents began his programme whilst in the process of requesting funding from the (then) local education authority. It was clear that the matter would proceed to tribunal and Alice and Ben tackled both the establishment of Sam's programme and their preparation for the political battle at the same time. The plan was for Sam to attend school on a part-time basis and receive specialist teaching at home for the remainder of the week. The programme began with a workshop attended by Sam's two tutors and his parents, and the school staff also attended for pertinent parts of the day. Sam was extremely fortunate with his tutors. One was a very gifted young woman – a qualified teacher – who was imaginative, insightful and very artistically talented. The other was a learning disability student from the University of Surrey – a (male) mature student who provided Sam with a balance to the almost overwhelmingly female influence in his educational world. In the company of these two people, along with Alice and Ben, Sam was to embark on an amazing journey of learning.

Early programming

Clearly, Sam was a little chap who already had many of the 'beginning' skills detailed in the Lovaas curriculum. For example, Sam had a reasonable understanding of language and spoke well, if oddly, and his ability to copy, to discriminate and to follow directions were not issues for his programme. He was able to do these things when he chose to – thus he did not need to be taught these things in the way other children on the programme might. Pre-intervention testing had indicated that (as suspected) Sam was functioning within the typical range on most measures, showing an above-average IQ score on standardised measures. However, testing also demonstrated that Sam's socialisation and play skills were delayed. Language assessments from around this time conclude that Sam's language skills (linguistic concepts, sentence structure, word structures) were very good – indeed, he was performing well above his age level – but that his pragmatic language skills were poor.

Another point that had to be taken into consideration when designing Sam's programme was keeping him motivated. Sam liked the stimulation provided by adult company, but his previous patterns of learning had demonstrated that his fragile self-esteem could not cope with tasks he considered too challenging. Thus, the work needed to be failure-proof while tackling his areas of need. In terms of daily motivation, the star stickers used at school were fairly successful with Sam and we discovered his liking for small toys – wind-up figures, stamps, jumping beans. A balance needed to be struck between motivating and stimulating Sam and the fatigue resulting from the effort he expended on learning. It was clear by this time that Sam's stamina was quite low and that any work with him needed to be at times when he was feeling well.

Thus, Sam's programme began, addressing areas of language pragmatics, the understanding of emotion, play, social sequencing, and some academic and school support skills.

Communication skills

The team worked on Sam's conversation skills, building up his ability to use his language skills in a social capacity. This began by enabling Sam to make an on-topic statement in response to his conversational partner. For example, his tutor would say, 'I like Snickers bars' and Sam would respond with, 'I like Mars bars'. He grasped this very quickly and within a matter of weeks was able to move this along to statements incorporating items from three categories. Thereafter, Sam also learned to use questions within conversation, which, combined with his ability to listen and stay on-topic, enabled much more daily conversation for Sam than previously. This ability had some positive spin-offs and Sam's eye contact improved, as did his willingness to engage in social greetings and small talk. Alice feels that this change in Sam's interaction had a profound effect on him. He was able to join in with daily exchanges and gain positive feedback from others in conversation. Sam has taken these skills much further and is now an interesting and interested companion. The team also worked on some language specifics, enabling Sam to understand and use language structures like 'before' and 'after', and 'either/or', which he mastered very quickly and was able to generalise with very little prompting.

Also of crucial importance was the work started at this stage on Sam's self-care skills. His initial test battery had demonstrated a significant shortfall in self-care skills – for example, Sam was unable to indicate that he needed to go to the toilet and a deterioration in his behaviour was the only sign of this need. Beginning to learn age-appropriate self-care skills made the time he spent at school less stressful for him and was a factor in his eventual re-integration to full-time schooling. These skills took a huge amount of time to master – he spent many hours practising coat fastenings – but Sam was very pleased to be able to do this like all the other children.

Play

In the past, play had been hugely problematic for Sam. By the time his programme started, he was interested in playing with others, but lacked the reciprocity and negotiation skills that would make this possible. Play with his brother or with children invited to the house usually ended in tantrums and tears, as Sam was rigid in his need to play his way. Sam knew how to play games; indeed, he had a good play repertoire. His difficulty was in playing with others. The programme began with some imaginative play, involving Sam and his tutor playing with some figures who would have some kind of adventure. The aims were to enable Sam to switch roles, to talk about the play as it progressed and to be able to take suggestions for changes to the play from his play pal. Again, Sam learned this very quickly and was, within the structure of the play, able to be much more flexible and accommodating. The next stage was to generalise this to play with his peers and also to enable more sharing of toys and activities.

Quite a large part of Sam's programme, as with all of the children, was play with his tutors during down time. Sam generally chose what to play, but the opportunity to spend time in play with skilled adults made an enormous difference to Sam's tolerance. He enjoyed board games and his ability to play these through and to stick to the rules improved hugely. Through these early months, he was much more able to begin and leave play activities appropriately and to listen to his play partner. He continued to enjoy rough and tumble play, and advice from the occupational therapist about exercises that would be helpful for Sam was accommodated within his programme.

Emotions

Given the range of difficulties faced by children with Sam's scatter of strengths and needs, it is often difficult to assess what they understand of their own and others' emotions. In light of this, it was decided to start with some very simple work on emotional recognition and expression. Initially, Sam identified emotions from others' expressions, photos and pictures (see Figure 3.1) and, with the aid of a mirror, made those expressions himself. Sam moved from here to recognising that situations cause emotions and was able to predict how someone would feel, when shown a picture or told a story about a particular situation. This was a major breakthrough for Sam, as he was able to identify with the children in the pictures and stories and thus began to show empathy for others.

sad

upset

tired

nervous

Figure 3.1   Some of Sam's learning aids from the early days

Sequencing

Part of the difficulty Sam had with managing his behaviour in the daily living environment was his inability to sequence his own actions or to predict the sequences of events around him. This part of Sam's programme began by having him arrange picture cards depicting a three-step story (e.g. two people talking beside a car, one of them getting into the car, the car moving away).

In parallel with this, work began on enabling Sam to predict outcomes of events and stories. Initially, familiar stories were used and Sam was asked, 'What happens next?' Later, novel stories were presented where Sam needed to use the information gained from the story and his imagination to predict events. This was initially quite challenging for him, but he was able to learn the principle from the particular examples he rehearsed. Thereafter, he was encouraged to think about his own actions, by means of his tutors asking him what he would do in particular circumstances. Clearly this kind of exercise can be made fun and Sam's sense of humour shone through in this work.

Later this work moved to having Sam sequence some actions and events, predicting what would happen next, his tutors then leading him into thinking through the proposed action. At this time, Sam was also thinking about the sequences he needed to follow to perform everyday tasks such as cleaning his teeth and getting dressed, which boosted his self-care skills enormously.

Academics

The remainder of Sam's 'at home' learning time was aimed at supporting his school placement through the rehearsal of skills he needed in that environment. Under the school's guidance, Sam revised phonics, using worksheets, puzzles and games, and began to do some basic spelling. This type of table work allowed the team to support Sam to work more independently, by giving him some closed-ended activities to work through on his own. Sam's ability to stay on task improved tremendously, even with background noise. This type of work also acted as a break for Sam from the intense one-to-one input necessary for the other aspects of his programme.

Circle time had been problematic for Sam at school and so this was rehearsed at home, using tutors and family members. At first, this was rather overwhelming for Sam and he would become very over-excited during these activities. However, within the first few months, he gained the ability to remain focused on the tasks and to participate well for up to ten minutes.

Mid-programming

Through the summer of 2000, Sam continued to make good progress in his areas of greatest need, attending school on a half time basis and working at home for 18 hours. While he continued to be co-operative at school and during his programme, Sam's increasing understanding led him to a greater awareness of, and ability to articulate, his difficulties. In the spring of 2000, he went through a very argumentative phase and some visual strategies were introduced to help him through this. Generally, his tolerance improved, particularly with his brother: he was keen to converse with Robert and they were able to play together more peaceably.

Communication

Having mastered the use of multiple statements and questions, Sam then learned how to listen to and summarise, and also to join a conversation. Previously, he had learned to say, 'Excuse me' when he wished to gain the attention of people who were already engaged in conversation, but the tone (loud, demanding) was rather inappropriate. Further work on refining Sam's volume and tone through this period worked well. Visual strategies were helpful here: Sam had a 'volume indicator' and learned to modulate his voice to reflect the numbers indicated on the thermometer. Recording Sam and his tutor speaking also worked well and gave him instant feedback on the tone of voice he was using. Enabling Sam to recognise when he was using an inappropriate tone took much rehearsal, and generalising these skills was also rather a slow process. However, by the end of the summer, his tone and pitch were much more reliable in day-to-day conversation.

Sam was also working on narrative at this point in his programme. The sequencing work he had previously undertaken boosted his ability here and he worked hard on telling a story with a beginning, middle and end. He also spent some considerable time on the skill of recalling and relating his own activities, although it is always hard to move children from the default response 'Nothing' to the question, 'What did you do in school today?' and Sam was no exception to this.

One area that presented tremendous difficulty both at school and at home was Sam's inability to ask for help. This was partly due to his personality – he just does like to do things for himself – but also because he had not rehearsed an appropriate vocabulary for these occasions. Thus, Sam was helped, through the use of verbal and visual prompts, to be able to ask for help as needed. Figure 3.2 shows the variety of types of help Sam might need and these props were kept in his pencil pot. In the same vein, Sam was also taught to use 'I don't understand' appropriately, as, again, being placed in a situation where he did not understand what was being asked of him led to deterioration in his behaviour.

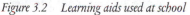

Figure 3.2   Learning aids used at school

Play and socialisation

The emphasis during this part of Sam's programme was on enabling him to play successfully with other children. He continued to learn skills with his tutors and to transfer these to play with his peers. For example, Sam learned some 'play phrases', that he could use, rehearsed these and then exercised this new skill with his peers. These were very helpful, both for him to keep the flow of play active but also to remind himself of the rules of appropriate behaviour – for example, if a peer lost a game, he could say, 'Never mind, we can play again later'.

Alice and Ben began to organise peer play sessions for Sam at this stage. Their past experiences of having children to their home had not been good, and so these were approached with some trepidation. However, as long as the dates were less than an hour and highly structured, some of the visits were very successful.

Academics

Occupational therapy involvement at this time was very helpful in giving advice on helping Sam to write comfortably. The recommendations of the therapist were built into Sam's programme and practised regularly. He continued to learn to read, following the lead set by the school.

Sam's ability to listen and predict had helped enormously with his co-operation at school. Circle time participation was much improved, as was Sam's ability to follow through tasks within the classroom environment. While one-to-one support in the school environment was maintained, notes from this period reveal that Sam was using his visual timetable independently to help navigate his way through the day and he would ask for help when needed.

Emotions

Sam's curriculum with regard to emotions at this stage was gleaned from a number of sources. Some of *Teaching Children with Autism to Mind Read* (Howlin, Baron-Cohen and Hadwin 1998) informed the approach, along with many of the ideas from Alison Schroeder's (1996) work and Freeman and Dake's (1997) language manual. Sam had little difficulty in grasping the concept that his behaviour had an emotional impact on others. He was able to predict what the impact might be (i.e. how the other person would feel as a result of his behaviour) and to suggest alternative behaviours if the initial behaviour were hurtful. However, he still failed to see why he should put others' needs before his own in some circumstances. I once showed him some 'consequences' pictures – one picture of a particular situation and three to choose from for an appropriate response to the situation. Sam's awareness was such that he was able to show me the 'right' picture and say, 'This is what I should do', and another, saying, 'But this is what I probably would do'. Thus Sam's team had to continue to provide extrinsic motivation for behaving appropriately, in the hope that Sam would 'grow into' a more moral stance toward his family and peers.

Later home learning

By the autumn of 2000, Sam had 'graduated' from the Lovaas programme. Whilst he continued to learn at home for some of his week (12 hours), he had covered the curriculum topics and the remainder of his work, as described above, was garnered from a number of sources. Sam continued to be willing to work at home, although the emphasis on issues that were, by definition, challenging to him meant that his tutors had to work very hard to maintain his motivation. At the same time, it was important to begin the process of ending Sam's home learning, as the aim was to have him in school full time by Easter of 2001. Two major issues formed the focus of work with Sam: self-regulation and play.

Behaviour

Whilst Sam's behaviour was generally much calmer and more predictable than previously, he was still very prone to feeling stressed and, resulting from this, losing his ability to use the skills he had. The consequence of this would be reversion to old behaviours of shouting and being tearful and demanding (see Gregory 2000). The increase in his school attendance led to Sam feeling tired and emotional on his return from school and he often needed up to an hour and a half on his own to regain his emotional equilibrium. He was, however, able to express how he felt and to divert himself from a behavioural breakdown by using some of the strategies he had learned. Jumping on the trampoline was a helpful device, as was taking a little 'chilling' time by watching the TV, talking issues through or having a hug with his mum. The ideas in Smith Myles and Southwick's (1999) text were lifesavers at this difficult time, helping everyone who worked with Sam to retain a perspective on his behaviour and our own responses to it.

The team had been addressing Sam's self-esteem, which was generally very low. In common with others on the autistic spectrum (see Fleisher 2003; Gillberg 2002), Sam had a need for perfection which had led him to think very poorly of himself when he did not meet his own very high standards. We had been helping Sam to recognise his strengths (see Figure 3.3) and to think about the areas in which he was not so strong in a much more positive way than previously. Fortunately, Sam's intellectual abilities were of great assistance here and we were able to tackle these emotional topics through his ability to understand the concepts presented. Some of these teaching approaches were adapted from McGinnis and Goldstein's (1990) work and, although they were helpful for Sam, their success was to some extent dependent upon his mood.

When tackling something that might be difficult, Sam learned the concept of 'trying' and the expression 'I can try', which have helped him enormously. The team spent time rewarding Sam for trying rather than achievement, as well as visibly failing to achieve some goals they set for themselves. I

– Things I am good at –

Sam's tutor
- Drawing
- Cooking
- Reading stories

Sam
- Swingball
- Writing stories
- History as a hobby

Figure 3.3　　An example of Sam's self-esteem work

was always struck at this time by how brave Sam was: his need for success was very strong and yet he was willing to 'try' at tasks at which he might fail – an awesome emotional undertaking for so small and fragile a child.

This work tied into a broader approach to encourage Sam to be more positive generally. He was rather a 'glass half-empty' child at this point and we used some strategies to encourage a more up-beat approach to events in his life. One of these is pictured in Figure 3.4 – Mr Positive and Mr Negative. We would use these characters in describing or discussing events that had happened and contrast the ways in which these two would think and talk about things. When Sam became negative about his work or school, he would be encouraged to reframe the situation to blend with Mr Positive's outlook.

Mr Positive   Mr Negative

Figure 3.4   Mr Positive and Mr Negative

Play

At times when Sam's general emotional well-being is suffering, his need to be in control re-emerges. Over the beginning of 2001, this presented as a revival of his previous competitiveness and an intolerance to losing games. To address this, the team revisited work on co-operative play, devising games and activities that required joint effort to achieve a goal, rather than winner–loser games.

His tutors also constructed a games book with Sam, which contained a variety of information and ideas about games (see Figure 3.5 for an example page). Social scripts, which emphasised the importance of co-operative play, of being a good sport and of both winning and losing graciously (see Figure 3.6), were included throughout the book. It also contained rules for the most popular games, and reference to these during play prevented arguments (Sam often tried to change rules in order to win). The book also contained a little history about games and some helpful definitions around cheating, luck, chance and so on. Because he had been involved in the creation of the games book, Sam was eager to use it as a guide in play and the strategy was very successful.

Games of Skill are Not Winning Games

Sometimes a game is about trying to do something that's difficult. This is called a game of skill. Here are some games of skill:

- Throwing a bean bag into a basket
- Kicking a ball into a goal
- Hitting a target with an arrow

I can play this kind of game by myself. I might count my hits, then try to beat my **own** best score. But I don't have to count. A game of skill isn't a winning game.

I can also play a game of skill with friends. Most children think it's fun to keep trying to do something that's difficult. I will try to remember that games of skill are not winning games. There's no need to keep score.

Figure 3.5   Extract from Sam's games book

Figure 3.6   Learning to lose

Full-time school

We were not able to assist Sam into full-time school by the Easter of 2001, due to his tiredness and difficulties with self-regulation. However, we did achieve this during the following term. Sam had one-to-one support in school and managed the transfer from primary to junior school very effectively. The junior school Sam attends is very large, but has a proactive and sensitive special needs staff group who are open to ideas from a variety of sources, and Sam has been well supported in this environment. He has been able to join in with most school activities, including the residential trips. He is about to transfer to secondary school – another huge transition for him.

Although Sam has not been receiving a home education programme per se since starting full-time school, his parents have continued to work on areas of difficulty with him, with the help of one of his ex-tutors. Generally, these difficulties crop up when Sam is physically low. Full-time school places an enormous strain on him, and he often cannot manage a whole term or half term and needs to spend some time at home before a school break (see Attwood 1998). Sometimes, when the strain becomes too much, Sam can lose his ability to negotiate and to use the strategies he has for managing his own behaviour and some difficult behaviour can resurface. His family has learned to renew the approaches we have previously taken to Sam's behaviour, updating these in accordance with his ability to understand precursors and consequences of behaviours. Thus, whilst Sam has made huge progress and learns alongside his peers in school, his autism continues to present him and his family with challenges.

A final note of interest here was that in the summer of 2003, Alice and Ben felt it was an appropriate time to tell Sam about his Asperger syndrome (see Jacobsen 2003). This was done in his home, with me leading Sam and the rest of his family through some games and discussion. Sam was given some pictures and simple explanations about the condition to look at and talk through, and I arranged to meet with him a few weeks later to follow up on any questions he had. This proved to be very successful for Sam. He took on board the fact that his difficulties were part of a broader pattern and that many other children and adults faced the same issues as him. He did go through a short phase of, 'I can't [whatever] because of my Asperger's' but this has now passed and he is ready to consider that many of the difficulties he faces are not 'his fault' and that he has special skills to counter balance the challenges he faces.

I am enormously optimistic for Sam. As he matures and his levels of self-awareness grow, I am confident that his intellectual abilities will enable him to develop reliable patterns of self-regulation and emotional equilibrium. He now has a very strong moral sense and knows how to make reparation if he has upset someone. He is very interested in others and, for example, recently gave his pocket money to a disaster relief agency in order to help other children. Whilst Sam has travelled a long way, he still finds the world a little disconcerting sometimes, but is very comfortable to say, 'I'm confused' and to take the help that is offered. He has become so much more himself over the years I have watched him learning and growing and I look forward to his development from a charming and engaging child to an equally engaging young man.

Below are some notes from Sam's brother Robert, outlining his reflections on having a brother who has undertaken a Lovaas programme.

Before programme

In infant school he came home at one o'clock because he was tired.

Touchy.

At holidays he was always by the TV, drawing, wrestling or bored.

When he was trying to stay at school all day, he came home tired and grumpy but would not rest.

I used to think he was a kind of 'short-term guy'. Meaning that he would be really bouncy, always wanting to wrestle me, then after a short while he would suddenly become really tired.

I got hit in bouncyness.

During programme

We used to play a game called 'Brother Wars' where me and Sam made rules so we didn't get hurt, then we wrestled on the sofa. He calmed down after that.

He liked to be squashed and still does.

He got a…of a lot more attention.

Mum was with him a lot more.

I couldn't go in the living room.

I thought he did work that was easy.

Like doing handwriting sheets, how is the face feeling, match voice to emotion.

I liked to join in art projects and enjoyed making a dinosaur viewing box.

Difference programme made

He's a lot more sensible and controlled.

He can now go to school full hours and he can recognise some emotions through body language.

He doesn't wrestle as much.

Joins in a lot more activity – games.

Can make friends easier.

Handwriting got better.

Mum was constantly saying 'What can I do so you don't feel left out?' A few times I felt that, but nowhere near as often as she asked me.

It's quite a big change, definitely for the better, now he's a lot more enjoyable for everyone.

It's a bit tricky going through the tutoring period, having people coming.

Quite fun – I could join sometimes – a bit annoying when I couldn't join.

I thought what Sam was doing was really easy.

Advice

It's a good idea but you have to be prepared for it.

It's a massive change, but when it's done you'll be glad everyone's a lot happier.

You'll go through some tough times, but when it's finished it will be worth it.

That's basically my opinion – based on fact.

References

Attwood, T. (1998) *Asperger's Syndrome: A Guide for Parents and Professionals.* London: Jessica Kingsley Publishers.

Fleisher, M. (2003) *Making Sense of the Unfeasible: My Life Journey with Asperger Syndrome.* London: Jessica Kingsley Publishers.

Fletcher, J. (1999) *Marching to a Different Tune: Diary about an ADHD Boy.* London: Jessica Kingsley Publishers.

Freeman, S. and Dake, L. (1997) *Teach Me Language: A Language Manual for Children with Autism, Asperger's Syndrome and Related Developmental Disorders.* Langley, Canada: Skf Books.

Gillberg, C. (2002) *A Guide to Asperger Syndrome.* Cambridge: Cambridge University Press.

Gregory, J. (2000) *Bringing Up a Challenging Child at Home: When Love is Not Enough.* London: Jessica Kingsley Publishers.

Hadcroft, W. (2004) *The Feeling's Unmutual: Growing up with Asperger Syndrome (Undiagnosed).* London: Jessica Kingsley Publishers.

Howlin, P., Baron-Cohen, S. and Hadwin, J. (1998) *Teaching Children with Autism to Mind Read.* Chichester: John Wiley and Sons Ltd.

Jacobsen, P. (2003) *Asperger Syndrome and Psychotherapy.* London: Jessica Kingsley Publishers.

McGinnis, E. and Goldstein, A.P. (1990) *Skillstreaming in Early Childhood.* Champagne, IL: Research Press.

Overton, J. (2003) *Snapshots of Autism: A Family Album.* London: Jessica Kingsley Publishers.

Schroeder, A. (1996) *Socially Speaking.* Cambridge: LDA Publishers.

Smith Myles, B. and Southwick, J. (1999) *Asperger Syndrome and Difficult Moments: Practical Solutions for Tantrums, Rage and Meltdowns.* Shawnee Mission, KS: Autism Asperger Publishing Co.

Williams, D. (1992) *Nobody Nowhere.* New York: Time Books.

Further reading

On Social Stories[TM]

Gray, C. (2000) *The New Social Story Book.* Arlington, TX: Future Horizons.

Chapter 4

Jack's Tale

Wavy Blue Cheese

Jack is now seven years old. He is generally an affable and laid-back little chap, who is great fun to be with. Jack enjoys lots of countryside activities: walking, fishing, horse-riding. He is less keen on indoor activities, but will watch a video with his brothers. Jack does not particularly desire interaction with other children but he is very sociable and communicative within his family and with adults close to him. Jack is very easy company – happy to hang out, easy to please.

Jack lives with his two brothers – one older and one younger than him – and his mum and dad in a rural town in Suffolk. When he was younger, Jack attended nursery and the same primary school as his brothers, in spite of the tremendous challenges presented by his autism. As the demands of the curriculum increased, this placement became inappropriate for Jack and he now (from academic Year 3) attends a specialist school in the local town, which he enjoys. Jack is an enthusiastic signer and a keen communicator.

The emergence of Jack's autism

As is often the case with children on the autistic spectrum, early photos of Jack reveal an apparently typically developing infant. He met early motor, play and communication milestones fully (Smith, Cowie and Blades 1997) and began to regress from the age of about 17 months old – just after he had the MMR (measles, mumps and rubella) vaccination. The debate over the possible link between MMR and autism has gained much media attention over the past few years, but Jack's parents – like many others – feel that the MMR vaccination was an important precipitating factor in the causation of Jack's autism. While they reject a simple cause and effect model for the implication of the vaccination in inducing autism, along with many other parents and professionals they

Jack as a baby with his older brother Tom

do feel that it is a crucial environmental factor for a child already genetically and physiologically vulnerable to autism (Blakemore-Brown 2002).

From the age of 18 months onward Jack began to lose skills: he became less verbal and less interactive, and his play became more stereotyped. Nicky and Paul (Jack's parents) were remarkably quick in recognising this change and acting upon it. Jack received a diagnosis of autistic spectrum disorder early in 1999 at the age of 23 months. Nicky and Paul were similarly decisive in providing early intervention for Jack, doing all the work necessary to start his programme in June of that year.

At the time (and much more clearly in retrospect) both Jack's parents and I felt we caught Jack 'on the way down' – that is, that his programme began before the full extent of his autism was apparent. Jack's progress through the curriculum varied in pace through the years of his intensive work but, in light of the developing course of his autism, he has acquired a remarkable range of skills and abilities.

Jack with his dear Laura, his nanny and one of his original tutors

Early programming

At the start of the programme, Jack presented as a very withdrawn little chap, who held a small train in each hand constantly. However, through the first weeks of intervention, he learned that he could put his trains in a basket beside the table, engage in a learning activity and then reclaim his trains. This was a big step forward as previous attempts to free Jack's hands for other activities had met with strong resistance. Another activity that took up quite a lot of Jack's time was book flipping – flicking the pages of a book over very quickly. During the early part of his programme, this behaviour was shaped into actually looking at books, starting with 'pop-up' and 'lift the flap' books.

Given that pre-intervention testing had revealed strong visual skills, some of the standard early programmes from the Lovaas curriculum were introduced in the first months of Jack's learning. Because he was very young, emphasis was placed on activities appropriate to his tender age: nursery rhymes, rough and tumble play, singing, and, during periods of play, cuddles, which were considerably longer than for an older child.

Jack progressed quickly through the visually based aspects of the programme. Having started in June, Jack was matching pictures by November. Similarly, he could copy pre-built block constructions by the end of his first six months of learning. Jack learned to copy actions at a slower pace, but was beginning to manage two-part imitation by Christmas.

Play

'Teaching play' may strike some readers as rather a contradiction in terms. For play to be play, surely it needs to be fun and to have an element of spontaneity? Can one teach this? Janet Moyles (1989) suggests a theoretical model for teaching play in the form of a play spiral. Within this, free play and directed play activities flow into each other, providing ever wider play experiences for the child. For a little child like Jack, who had very few play behaviours, this teaching needed to be much more overt and directed than with a typically developing child. For example, individual play behaviours – such as pushing the car along or twisting the knob on a pop-up toy – had to be taught through discrete trial teaching. Once Jack had mastered the skills these were transferred to his down-time play. Jack engaged in them with his tutor; the reinforcement of the tutor's encouragement was gradually faded to allow Jack to play with the toy alone and (we hope!) spontaneously. It is sometimes difficult to comprehend just how much needs to be taught that we take for granted will just be acquired in the typically developing child. However, the principle remains the same – providing opportunities for play development through guidance, teaching and just having fun with the child.

Pre-intervention, 'play' for Jack was lining up his trains or other manipulable objects. Through the programme Jack learned to play with a wide variety of toys but his 'free choice' remained quite limited. Throughout his childhood thus far, he has homed in on a few activities or toys at any one time rather than being flexible and free-ranging in his play behaviour. Nonetheless, the changes in his play behaviour were most marked in the early stages of the programme as Jack's newly acquired play skills served as a vehicle for more constructive play with his older brother and neighbouring children.

Communication

At the beginning of Jack's programme he still had some words from his fading and shrinking vocabulary. These were nurtured in a fun way, through games, songs and rhymes. At the same time, we worked on building up Jack's vocabulary receptively and this was rather slow work at first – it took two months for Jack to master six new words. Jack also had some difficulty during the first six months of his programme with non-cued instructions, as well as social activities such as waving. In relation to his speech, Jack was whispering rather than using his voice by December of 1999 and so a no-pressure approach was taken to vocal work.

Socialisation

The 'when' question in relation to nursery/pre-school attendance is one that poses difficulties for the families of pre-school children on any home education programme. On one side of the debate is the question of what is the purpose in sending a child to nursery who has no or few skills to access the play and socialisation activities on offer. The child will be physically present but in all other ways 'absent' from the nursery. It is suggested instead that the child should attend when he or she has sufficient skills and motivation to benefit from the experience. The Peach website (www.peach.org.uk) suggests that children should have sufficient skills before entering nursery. On the other side of the debate is the argument that children need exposure to other children and even brief, unintentional contacts at nursery can be learning experiences for the child. As the child gains more skills through learning at home, familiarity with the environment will facilitate generalisation of these skills to the nursery setting.

Jack's parents were of the latter opinion and he attended a nursery throughout his pre-school years. For the first six months this was a small, local, voluntarily run nursery. Jack (as is typical of him) was happy enough to attend and whoever accompanied him from home made opportunities for him to interact with the other children. Whilst Jack was co-operative with these games and activities and never objected to the other children approaching or directing him, he did not seek out interaction. At home, he was keen to be with his brothers and the neighbourhood children. Whenever a group of children were playing in the garden, Jack would be near them, at the periphery of the group but the impetus for interaction (despite the skills Jack had acquired in this area) still needed to come from another child or be provided by an adult.

Behaviour

Throughout his life thus far, Jack's typical equanimity has been occasionally interrupted by periods of rather challenging behaviour. Some of these appear to start without cause, although for others a clear trigger factor can be found. They last anywhere from a few days to a couple of months. These periods are very distressing for Jack, his family and those working with him, not least because this behaviour is so unlike his usual 'cool'. The first of these periods occurred in September of 1999 when Jack showed some aggression to his brothers. This was managed behaviourally and diminished quickly. In November, some biting behaviour appeared during cuddles and rough and tumble play. Again, this was managed by a short withdrawal of attention and interaction, and faded away.

Throughout 1999 and 2000 considerable attention within the autism world was paid in the specialist (and other) press to apparently efficacious effects of secretin for children with autism (for example, *Daily Express* 1999; Hovarth *et al.* 1998). Nicky and Paul felt they would like to try this approach with Jack and he had his first dose of secretin in November of 1999, repeated six weeks later. This drug did have an effect on Jack's behaviour. After both administrations of the drug Jack displayed some aggression (indeed, the administration of the drug coincided with one of the periods of aggression mentioned above), was more interactive and was more social. The desired effects were short-lived, however, and Nicky and Paul felt that the positive effects were outweighed by the negative. Later (from 2001) Jack took homeopathic secretin, although withdrawal of this in 2003 did not appear to alter his awareness, skills or behaviour (see Ferrin 1999).

A day out

Mid-programming

Throughout the programme, Nicky and Paul also investigated the possible physiological aspects of Jack's condition. Test results suggested that Jack had a candida problem and he had a course of medication to address this. This did not bring about the physical effects sometimes reported for the drug and neither did it have an effect on his psychological or social functioning. Jack had been gluten- and casein-free (Le Breton 2001) since 1999 and through-out the mid-programming stage (to 2001) Jack was 'challenged' occasionally with gluten or casein foods. The results of either intentional or accidental (e.g. consuming a mouthful of play dough) challenges were the same: a loss of ability to focus and concentrate, emotional instability and loss of communica-tion and socialisation skills and motivation (Seroussi 2000). Thus, as is often the case, whilst the withdrawal of these foods from Jack's diet had not had an immediate impact on his behaviour, they clearly were detrimental to his ability to learn effectively. (Later, by 2003, however, Jack appeared to have built up a tolerance for these foods and was able to eat them with no effect on his skills and behaviour. This was a huge joy to Jack and he has developed into a bit of a cheese connoisseur.)

Communication

Over this period of time Jack began to show his ability to learn words inciden-tally. He was able to point to named objects or activities in books that he had not been taught directly. This ability sprang, I think, from the very consistent and thorough teaching Jack had through these years in acquiring a large noun vocabulary, adjectives, verbs and some prepositions. It is difficult to over-emphasise the importance of repetition and consistency in enabling children to learn (Leaf and McEachin 1999), but Jack's team were expert at judging where difficulties were cropping up, at altering the presentation of materials accordingly and, crucially, at keeping Jack interested.

Sadly, Jack's use of his voice faded away. He began initially to lose final sounds in words (e.g. 'ca' rather than 'cat') and by October 2000 the initial sounds also faded (so 'cat' became 'a'). Particularly in the light of the progress he was making with other aspects of language and across his programme, this loss of his ability to use his voice for communication was very sad for Jack, his parents and the adults working with him. We had begun using PECS (Picture Exchange Communication System) in a fairly low-key fashion with Jack pre-viously, but this now became his main means of expressive communication. The cognitive requirements for using the system presented no challenges to

Jack – he was very able to differentiate icons, find his PECS book and make up a sentence. The difficulty we did have was in encouraging Jack to use it as a communication rather than just a requesting system.

Play

Throughout 2000 Jack's team continued to expand his play repertoire. He was happy to engage in interactive play with his tutors and, for a short time in the early part of the year, was quite intrigued by the etch-a-sketch. Jack learned some symbolic play with small figures and, when prompted, would continue this play in short, novel scenarios. Despite this, Jack never engaged in symbolic play spontaneously – I always felt he didn't see the point. He continued to enjoy construction play and would play board games (picture lotto) and turn-taking games such as 'Pop-up Pirates' and 'Hungry Hippos'. However, the situation with regard to Jack's spontaneous play with other children continued as previously. Despite using the usual strategies, he remained aloof from the other children at nursery. He continued to be co-operative with structured play but drifted away from the others as soon as the structure was loosened.

Socialisation

In 2000 Jack moved to attend a larger nursery in the town, which his brother had attended. The staff at this nursery were positive, welcoming and enthusiastic. Prior to Jack's start, the staff welcomed all the support offered to enable them to provide Jack with a good experience of nursery. As his supervisor, I visited on a regular basis to observe Jack and, on these days, the staff would spend their lunch hours having some teaching input and discussing how to enable Jack to gain as much as possible from his time with them.

Jack was accompanied by one of his tutors to nursery and his or her role was to facilitate Jack's involvement in nursery activities. As is characteristic of Jack, he would do as cajoled or told by the more dominant (usually girl) children but did not initiate interaction. He particularly enjoyed the seesaw but needed heavy prompting to approach another child for play, even though he knew how to do this. This unwillingness to engage with other children was a source of huge frustration to all of Jack's education team, as setting up opportunities, manipulating the environment, rewarding even the slightest sign of interest in others were all met with Jack's typical nonchalance. However, Jack enjoyed his time at this nursery and took part in the Christmas drama production, much to everyone's delight.

Behaviour

Jack was quite happy through the early part of this period. He went through a phase of pushing his hands into his nappy, which was tackled by keeping him busy and the purchase of several pairs of dungarees. At nursery, Jack was generally quite passive, although he could be a little noisy during story time and was not so good at waiting for his snack. He hit rather a difficult phase in the middle of the year with an increase in tantrumming, which again was managed using an ignore–redirect approach (see Wolverson 2003). Crucially, it was Jack's behaviour that was being ignored in using this strategy, not Jack. Thus, the people around him were acknowledging him, drawing him into a constructive activity and reinforcing him heavily for the non-tantrum behaviour. While following through on this type of seemingly simple strategy can be very challenging, the behavioural basics have always been reliable at stormy times with Jack.

A more complex problem arose for the first time during 2001: Jack began to get very distressed – almost inconsolable – if his mum left the house without him. We saw this pattern appear twice more over the following couple of years, with a different focus for Jack's attachment: Jack's dad and older brother were involved in later appearances of the same behaviour. The approach that one would take with a typically developing child of reassurance and distraction were ineffective for Jack and many different strategies were tried to reduce his distress. Foreshadowing the departure appeared to help a little, as did the use of a picture timetable to illustrate when Mum would be back. However, this was an upsetting time for Jack and those working with him.

Academics

Jack made great steps forward as we tackled some academic work with him as a preparation for school. He had been doing some artwork throughout his programme and we began some more focused colouring work with attention to his pencil grip. Jack learned to recognise numbers and letters and by mid-2001 was able to write a few words. Jack's knowledge of the world also grew during this time and he learned to sequence, and what were the functions of objects, opposites and so on. Jack was also acquiring information incidentally, as a result of his greatly improved receptive language skills.

Jack's writing has always been a little 'wild' and still tends to be a gross rather than fine motor activity. He has sometimes liked writing and, at other times, actively tried to avoid it – this latter occurring when the demands for accuracy increased.

School

In 2002 Jack transferred to the local primary school's reception class along with many of his peers from nursery. Being known by the children was a huge benefit to Jack as he was able to adjust to the demands of the classroom (albeit part time) without a new set of children. Jack managed reception class quite well – the free-flowing activity at school must have seemed quite relaxed to Jack who was still having some fairly structured teaching at home – Jack has always been quite happy, if unfocused, in unstructured environments. We continued to maintain links between the home and school strands of Jack's education through the presence of a home tutor as shadow and monthly visits from the programme supervisor.

Growing up

Later programming

By definition, an early intensive programme aims to decrease the 'home' element and increase the 'school' element of the child's education as soon as possible. Throughout 2002 (Jack's Year 1) we tried on several occasions to increase his school attendance but this was not successful from the perspective of Jack's well-being. Through the year we did not manage full-time school (in fact we achieved a maximum of seven out of the ten available sessions) and eventually realised that the demands at school were just too great for Jack at this stage of his development.

Communication

Jack's reluctance to use his PECS for social communication continued to be a stumbling block in advancing his communication skills. During 2002 we introduced some Makaton signs to Jack and this opened a whole new realm of communication to him. He acquired the first signs very quickly and, over the months following its introduction, acquired signs at an exponential rate. We began this work by teaching signs in a discrete trial format, but later Jack was able to learn them in a much more natural fashion. He was keen to know the signs for things he came across in books and in life and would make up his own signs when a conventional one was not known. Jack is extremely inventive: the title of this chapter comes from his explanation of exactly what he wanted from the fridge, as he didn't know the sign for Gorgonzola!

Play

Jack's tutors continued to target new play skills and maintain his existing ones remarkably well considering the lack of encouragement Jack gave them. He would, as previously, co-operate with games and activities with his brothers, peers and tutors, but would much prefer to be 'non-engaged'. This posed rather a dilemma during school playtimes, as they represented an ideal opportunity for structured peer play. However, the stresses of focusing for lessons, listening, writing, and so on in the classroom meant that Jack was keen to have a run-around alone at break times and it was generally felt that he needed some 'free' time in the same way as the other children. Jack's play interests continued to change – he was very keen on Harry Potter at one point and this enabled some extended figurine play – never, alas, spontaneously.

Socialisation

As may be gathered from the section above, Jack's interest in children outside the family did not increase during this time. He was very happy at home, always involved in family activities and keen to be near his brothers. Attempts to engage him more directly with other children were met with his pliable acquiescence but no real enjoyment.

It had begun to be apparent to Nicky, Paul and me that the need we felt to have Jack play with other children was just that – our need. We faced the reality that giving Jack the skills, opportunities and rewards for engaging with other children, through teaching, did not necessarily lead to a position where this engagement was something he actively desired. Jack's family and friends continue to provide opportunities for social interaction for him and to teach age-appropriate skills so that, should Jack decide he wants to engage with others, he has the wherewithal to do so.

Behaviour

Jack had had a fairly settled time through 2002 and into the beginning of 2003 but it was the return to school after the summer break that saw a huge deterioration in Jack's ability to maintain his emotional and behavioural equilibrium. This began in June when Jack's sleep pattern became very erratic and his obsession with family members returned. Again, these issues were managed behaviourally but Jack was unable to contain his emotion at school. During September and October he became very distressed and angry. Consequently, he spent less time at school and at home strategies were introduced to give Jack more control over his environment and more understanding of appropriate ways to express frustration and anger.

During this time, Jack also developed a pervasive self-stimulatory behaviour – he liked to collect fluff and watch it as he threw it into the air. This behaviour grew quickly until it was taking up a large proportion of Jack's non-engaged time. We decided to contain the behaviour geographically – it was permissible in one particular place and with the fluff already there in his fluff box – but not in other places. Initially, this meant that the adults with Jack needed to be very vigilant and every time he acquired some fluff, he was directed to the 'fluff' area in the house, and to the fluff already in his box (extracted from the tumble drier and thus top quality for this activity). Jack was left to play with his fluff, an activity that became much shorter in duration, and then redirected into more constructive activity. Jack soon realised that there was a particular place for this activity – the 'Fluff Protocol' was successful in limiting this behaviour and enabling more constructive activity at other times.

School

Jack spent much of this term at home, during which time Nicky and Paul looked for a more specialist educational placement for him. It was apparent that, despite Jack's cognitive abilities, the social and language demands of the mainstream placement were too challenging for him at this point. Clearly, in terms of both age and ability he had moved beyond the 'early intervention' stage and Jack's home education altered considerably during this period to reflect that. During his time at school, his work at home had focused on issues specific to his autistic spectrum disorder, aimed at supporting his main educational placement. Now, the focus shifted to providing Jack with knowledge about the world he lives in and skills that will enable him to be more inde-

Jack now

pendent. He enjoyed the weekly trip to the library to find books on that particular week's topic and this new calm was reflected in Jack's behaviour, which improved over the months he spent at home.

Fortunately, Nicky and Paul found an excellent specialist school in their local town and Jack now attends this on a full-time basis. Jack is very happy at school and has settled well into the same weekly routine as his brothers.

In conclusion

I am loath to close this chapter. Over the years, Jack has presented his parents and me with some tough challenges, many moments of delight and on-going pleasure in his company. The early learning Jack undertook has given him a sound skills base for the rest of his life – he has an evolving communication system, good self-care skills, basic literacy and numeracy, and play and socialisation skills, should he choose to use them. On this last note, I feel that, despite the fact that Jack does not yet use these skills, we have given him a choice. Had he not learned to play with others, ask and answer social questions and so on, we would not know that Jack actually chooses not to do these things at present.

I wish I could see what the future holds for Jack, but, of course, I cannot. However, I hope that all the work he undertook will be of benefit to him in whatever life offers him. I was honoured to work with Jack and his family. Below, Jack's mum presents her perspective of the Lovaas programme, which, I hope, may be of help to other parents and enlightening to professionals in the fields of autism education.

A mother's perspective

My son, Jack, was diagnosed with autistic spectrum disorder (ASD) four days before his second birthday. In retrospect, I believe that we were fortunate in getting such an early diagnosis because Jack's autism was so profound and his decline so dramatic. At 16 months, Jack was a happy, engaging and sociable child; at two years he was withdrawn, obsessive and showing signs of severe impairment. The diagnosis confirmed my suspicions but I took it very hard. I had had some experience of people with autism during time spent training as a nurse, and the memory of those experiences terrified me. I pictured my son in his adulthood, wandering aimlessly around some day centre, simply existing rather than living. I imagined him passive, without a voice and, most distressing for me, disrespected.

I would not be reassured by professionals, family and friends that everything would be OK and that I would cope: I wanted my son to have a real life. I
also worried endlessly about the effect Jack's ASD would have on his brothers
and on our family's future. A frantic literature search did little to alleviate my
worries and much of the material I read contributed to my feelings of despair. I
eventually read about Lovaas in a magazine article and sought out more information on the approach.

The Lovaas approach appealed in many ways. It seemed, first and
foremost, to be entirely sensible in nature. The intensity of the approach
seemed crucial to me. I felt that I was not going to help my son with
anything that was half-hearted or sporadic. Whilst there were very encouraging claims in terms of potential recovery, Lovaas didn't suggest that I
could 'cure' my child with love or 'holding'. I already loved him and felt
strongly that we could continue to love him while applying this intensive
behavioural approach to address his difficulties. The fact that the approach
was supported by credible research strengthened my resolve. My husband
and I discussed our decision with Jack's paediatrician who advised us to
'wait and see' how Jack developed. This advice was contrary to the prevail-
ing research which recommended early intervention as crucial to the
optimal development of children with ASD. 'Wait and see' was not an option
– I knew what kind of future my child faced.

The statementing process

Having made the decision to adopt the Lovaas approach we set about establishing the programme. Securing a provider turned out to be the most
straightforward part of the process for us. Dr Anderson was able to schedule
the start of Jack's programme for June that year – just three months after his
initial diagnosis. Of course a Lovaas programme is very expensive and our
battle to secure funding began.

We requested that Jack undergo statutory assessment in order to secure a
statement of special educational needs (see Friel, Friel and Hay 1996). This,
we hoped, would allow for the provision of the programme through the local
education authority (LEA). The assessment and statementing processes were
tedious and time-consuming and resulted in the LEA prescribing a minimal
and unsatisfactory provision for Jack. We then began an appeal to the Special
Educational Needs (SEN) Tribunal.

Jack's programme began months before the funding issues were resolved
and this had serious financial implications. I had given up my part-time

nursing post and we were managing on one modest wage with three young children – we certainly did not have the thousands of pounds needed to run the programme. We needed to raise some funds and my husband and I found this to be one of the most stressful and, at times, humiliating aspects of the whole experience. We had some welcome donations from family members but a significant amount of the cash was raised by the parents of Jack's first Lovaas tutor who made tremendous efforts on his behalf. We used Jack's Disability Living Allowance, raided the children's fairly insignificant savings plans and embarked on a less than insignificant journey into debt!

Eventually our SEN Tribunal date came and, for a couple of thousand pounds, we were represented by a barrister who presented more or less the same information to the tribunal as I had given to the LEA many months before. The tribunal named the Lovaas programme as the appropriate educational approach for Jack and the LEA was instructed to fund the programme.

Running the programme

Jack's initial tutors were ourselves and Laura, a 17-year-old girl who had just completed a nursery nurse course and who had had some contact with our family. Five years on Laura is still involved, to some extent, in Jack's programme and has become a firm family friend and one of Jack's favourite people. Most other tutors were students from the local college. Newspaper adverts for tutors were expensive and of limited success. What worked for us was the personal recommendation of existing tutors who felt they knew someone perfect for the job. We've ticked over quite nicely like this with tutors staying for an average of two years. Our tutors have been a hardworking, reliable and imaginative bunch!

Before making a commitment to employing a potential tutor, I would suggest a trial period of a few weeks supervised work with Jack. One of the most significant indicators for a successful placement was whether the tutor and the family felt comfortable together. The programme required that Jack's tutors work with him for about 30 hours per week. They were so much a part of our lives that we simply had to like them and they had to be confident with Jack and relaxed within our family environment.

Although the programme itself demands a certain amount of organisation and facilitation, its benefits to our family have far exceeded its demands. From the outset, the Lovaas programme actually allowed us to have more time with our other children. Even though we initially covered many of the therapy hours, our down time could be devoted to our other children (and the household chores). We were confident that Jack was not being 'babysat' by his tutors. He was being educated and stimulated by a small group of people committed to helping him to achieve his potential. The programme also added structure and routine to our lives which I'm sure helped us tremendously with our confidence in our ability to cope.

Throughout the years since diagnosis Jack has demonstrated some difficult and at times distressing behaviours. It has been of enormous benefit to us that we have always been able to receive immediate advice and support from Jack's Lovaas supervisor. If we had relied on access to the usual overstretched resources, I'm sure we would have had to wait some considerable time for any help at all. I think it is important not to under-estimate the value of this level of support. Parents can feel pretty helpless when faced with bizarre and difficult to manage behaviours and this helplessness must contribute to feelings of depression. Having access to emotional support and practical advice has ensured that we have rarely felt that things were desperate or out of control. Considering the severity of Jack's autism, I think that this is more than noteworthy.

Effects on the family

For me personally, Jack's Lovaas programme has been very empowering. I have seen that there are workable strategies for almost every problem and feel more confident in my ability to devise my own strategies to help Jack's future to be as I think he would want it. I am encouraged to be proactive on Jack's behalf because I have seen that there are others who believe children like Jack are worth all the time and effort we can give them.

Jack has two brothers: Tom, 17 months older, and Harry, 14 months younger. Given the small age gaps and the fact that Jack's intervention started so early, they have lived with the Lovaas programme for as long as they can remember. Obviously they are aware that Jack gets lots of intense and individual attention and this may have some impact. However, I think that, without the programme, Jack would require just as much attention, but perhaps in a less positive way. I think that he would have more difficult behaviours and these would have become more entrenched and thus have significant consequences for our family life.

There are times when I am concerned that Tom and Harry hear Jack being praised and congratulated for some seemingly small achievement whilst they are consistently achieving more with only a fraction of the immediate reward.

When I try to explain the reasons for this, however, they respond with a 'yeah, we know that – what are you fussing about' attitude. I think that they enjoy Jack's achievements and that they like that the tutors think Jack is 'cool'. I also believe that the consistently positive approach to Jack by his tutors helps his brothers be very accepting of him. Even when he's having a very difficult day, they boys will simply state, 'Better steer clear; Jack's grumpy today'.

Effects on Jack

While the benefits and demands of the programme on the family are important, it is, of course, the effect on the child with autism that is crucial here. We had read of children who had reached some kind of 'recovery' following a Lovaas programme and, if I'm honest, that is what I yearned for in the early days. However, Jack isn't recovered or even anything near it. He remains non-verbal, has little interest in other children and can be quite demanding, but I still feel that he has achieved so much and benefited enormously from his years of intervention.

In the early Lovaas days, Jack was a high flyer, mastering skills rapidly; but he would take two steps forward and at least one step back. I feel in retrospect that his regressive autism was still just kicking in during his second and third year, and that we had a long way down to go. Some people's initial enthusiasm for the work quickly waned when he didn't manage to sustain his initial rapid rate of progress. Our resolve to continue to help him strengthened – we soon realised that Jack was at the more severe end of the spectrum so consequently he would need more of our help.

Although different communication strategies are seemingly available for anybody to use with their child, it is very difficult for a family to effectively adopt them without some additional structure in place. Even assuming the child's speech and language therapist is able to teach the skills required for a communication system, and ours was not, making the opportunities to practise those skills can be very difficult. The Lovaas programme enabled us to try different strategies with Jack in a way in which he understood: by presenting information using the discrete trial method. With Jack's tutors, it gave us the resources to practise acquired skills at frequencies far in excess of those we could otherwise have managed, and with the skills of our supervisor we are able to develop Jack's signing in a purposeful way.

The programme has allowed Jack to demonstrate the disparity between his outward self and his real self. By this, I mean that Jack is to be one of those children who are so severely affected by their condition that it is difficult to determine their actual understanding of the world.

Finally, the programme has helped Jack to develop a flexibility in his approach to life. He has a stable group of tutors with changing membership who provide a consistent teaching approach each with their individual style. When he begins to demonstrate any rigidity it is quickly recognised and strategies are adopted to avert a major problem. This makes Jack a lot easier to live with and therefore makes for a happier and less stressed-out family. We, of course, have difficult days, Jack is prone to the occasional aggressive outburst, but we are confident enough in our skills as a team (and that includes Jack) to know we'll get through a problem and out the other side!

We are very close to the end of our programme and it is clear that Jack is and always will be at the severe end of the autistic spectrum. We feel that we have given Jack lots of tools and that he is using them as he is able. I'm glad that we tried so hard for him and that he tries so hard for us.

References

Blakemore-Brown, L. (2002) *Reweaving the Autistic Tapestry: Autism, Asperger Syndrome and ADHD*. London: Jessica Kingsley Publishers.

Daily Express (1999) 'Wonder drug that brings hope to 90% of autistic children.' *Daily Express*, 19 August.

Ferrin, N. (1999) 'The homeopathic treatment of autism.' In *The Autism File*, www.autismfile.com/articles/issue1_05.htm (accessed 8 December 2006).

Friel, H., Friel, J. and Hay, D. (1996) *Special Educational Needs and the Law*. London: Sweet and Maxwell.

Hovarth, K., Stefatos, G., Sokolski, K., Watchel, R., Nabors, L. and Tildon, J. (1998) 'Autistic behaviour and secretin.' *Journal of the Association for Academic Minority Physicians*, 9 (1), 9–15.

Leaf, R. and McEachin, J. (eds) (1999) *A Work in Progress – Behavioural Management Strategies and a Curriculum for Intensive Behavioural Treatment of Autism*. New York: DRI Books.

Le Breton, M. (2001) *Diet Intervention and Autism: Implementing the Gluten Free and Casein Free Diet for Autistic Children and Adults – A Practical Guide for Parents*. London: Jessica Kingsley Publishers.

Moyles, J. (1989) *Just Playing: The Role and Status of Play in Early Childhood*. London: Open University Press.

Seroussi, K. (2000) *Unravelling the Mystery of Autism and Pervasive Developmental Disorder*. New York: Simon and Schuster.

Smith, P., Cowie, H. and Blades, M. (eds) (1997) *Understanding Children's Development*. London: Blackwell.

Wolverson, M. (2003) 'Challenging behaviour.' In B. Gates (ed.) *Learning Disabilities: Toward Inclusion*. London: Elsevier Science.

Chapter 5

David's Tale

I'm Not David, I'm Woody

David is now nine years old. He is a lovely child who always looks very laid back, and this style is reflected in his speech. I always feel that David finds adults he doesn't know well slightly tedious, but that he humours us when he needs to. He lives in a city just outside London with his parents, older sister and younger brother. He has recently become much closer to his siblings, and this is mirrored in an increasing interest in having friends to his home to play. He enjoys using the computer, reading books and watching TV and videos, and is currently very interested in the theatre. He loves children's theatre and is involved with a performing arts group, where he enjoys singing, acting and drama. He is very happy to follow direction, but improvisation is still rather challenging for him. David has an active sense of humour and is good company.

David has attended mainstream education throughout his programme. Pre-intervention, attendance at a local nursery was very difficult, due to his behaviour: David would shout and tear displays from the walls, and was rather a disruptive force in the classroom. However, home education alongside a pre-school placement has been very successful for him. He moved at the appropriate time from nursery to the local mainstream primary school. Through the years, his attendance at school has increased as his home education hours have decreased and he is currently in Year 4 of the local junior school. David has one-to-one support in school but is becoming increasingly independent within this environment.

Pre-intervention

It was apparent to David's parents, Ruth and Ben, that David had some difficulties for some time prior to diagnosis. When he was two years old, in 1997, his parents thought he might have a hearing problem, as he was unresponsive to the kinds of stimuli to which one would expect a small child to react. However, David's hearing proved to be good and a speech and language delay was diagnosed and language therapy started. He was described as being very difficult to work with at this stage and progress was painfully slow. David was then referred to the local child development centre where he was seen several times and it was generally felt that he had a communication disorder. Starting nursery enabled input from the pre-school advisory teacher from the local education authority, although at this time, David's condition was becoming even more apparent, with disruptive behaviour becoming a regular and frequent part of his day.

At this point, the 'opportunity class' aimed at meeting David's needs was offered and Ruth accompanied David to this. In the mean time Ruth and Ben had attended a language course (the Hanen programme) and David began to make some small progress. However, there was a lack of consistency between the different learning environments and approaches David was receiving at this time, which caused him some confusion. His behaviour continued to deteriorate, with tantrums, sleep problems, self-stimulatory behaviour – David would run from one corner of the ground floor of the house to the other – proving problematic. Particularly challenging was David's habit of removing his clothes and screaming and fighting when Ruth tried to replace them. A report from the nursery staff concerning this time reflects much the same pattern: wandering around and tantrumming if prevented; aggression to other children; inability to sit for communal activities and destructive behaviours.

The escalation of David's difficulties led his parents to pursue the matter of diagnosis further and David was first diagnosed in the US in August 1998. This was confirmed by the local children's services in October of that year.

Beginning home education

David has been very fortunate, as (in common with the other children in the book) the love and dedication of his parents has enabled him to pursue this course of very specialist education, which has suited him very well. David's parents feel very fortunate to have been in a position where they could afford to start the programme independently – an option not available to all parents. Further, they feel that a crucial factor in David's success has been having Ruth at home to oversee the programme and generalise the skills David has learned. David's parents appreciate the fact that not all parents are in a position to be able to have one parent at home while the other goes out to work and feel blessed to have been able to afford to do this.

In seeking a more coherent approach to David's pre-school education, Ruth attended a PEACH conference to find out about the Lovaas approach and was impressed, particularly by the video material shown there on other children who had undertaken the programme. Ruth and Ben started on the long trail of discovery that many parents undertake at this already difficult juncture and found talking to other parents most helpful in deciding on the best course of action in assisting David. Despite the rhetoric in the field, it is generally agreed that much more research is needed concerning the efficacy of all different types of intervention (see Jordan, Jones and Murray 1998). Ruth felt that applied behavioural analysis (ABA) approaches had a sound theoretical and research base and, perhaps as importantly, that the research in this area was on-going and proactive. Thus, the family decided to begin a Lovaas programme for David and was able to arrange this for December of 1998.

Additional intervention

A debate continues in the ABA community over the concomitant use of these approaches and other types of intervention. The logic is easy to follow: if a child is on a gluten-free/casein-free diet and in receipt of Lovaas intervention, what proportion of success or failure do we accredit to each approach? Thus, purists would opt for a 'Lovaas-only' intervention. However, as I commented in Chapter 1, it is the child and family who are central in this learning process and so many practitioners are comfortable with dietary manipulation alongside an ABA programme.

Ruth and Ben have provided a strong and thorough home education programme for David. They have also been advocates for applied behavioural analysis, supporting other parents and involving themselves heavily in the local and national political arena in the struggle for appropriate education for children on the autistic spectrum. As well as addressing David's condition through education, they feel that there is a strong bio-medical component to David's autism and have addressed this over the years in parallel with his home learning programme.

David has been on a gluten- and casein-free diet since 1999 (for more information see www.autismmedical.com). Whilst David has always been fairly co-operative with this dietary regime, juggling different food requirements can be an additional difficulty in running a home (Le Breton 2001).

David was challenged with some foods containing gluten and casein in 2003 and it took two months for the effects of this to become apparent. Over the two months of taking these foods, David became physically ill with typical gut symptoms, was very excitable and developed the classic red ear. However, the most worrying aspect of the changes was the loss of skills David showed: he lost a lot of interaction and communication and showed a concomitant increase in self-stimulatory behaviour and difficulties in self-monitoring and control. The video-talk, previously a pervasive behaviour, which had diminished considerably, reappeared strongly and David was back in the position of being disruptive in school assemblies. David also had a recurrence of sleep problems and the combination of these alarming factors led Ruth and Ben to reinstate the previous dietary restrictions. As a result of this, within another two months David's condition improved again and his parents felt that he was back to where he had been before the dietary infractions took place.

Another approach that David's family has investigated is that of the possible involvement of mercury in the systems of children and adults on the autistic spectrum. This is a relatively new area of research in the field and as yet has attracted little attention in the UK. Part of the difficulty may be that it is, by definition, connected to the MMR debate (mentioned in Chapter 4), which has become rather a vicious battleground within the last few years. However, it is suggested that some children may be genetically predisposed to sensitivity to heavy metals (McCandless, Binstock and Zimmerman 2003). Buttar (2004) cites Holmes, Blaxill and Haley's 2003 study which demonstrated that autistic children have much lower levels of mercury in their hair samples than typically developing children, suggesting a reduced detoxification ability. It would further appear that treatment to enhance the children's ability to detoxify results in amelioration of the child's autism. The children in Dr Buttar's study were treated with DMPS (dimercaptopropane sulfanate) which can have some distressing side effects and thus many parents rule out this approach. However, McCandless *et al.* (2003) refer to a new protocol for heavy metal toxicity involving nutrient and mineral supplementation. Although no trials have been run, anecdotal reports of the efficacy of the approach are favourable. It is this approach that Ruth and Ben have followed with David and this treatment is on-going.

Early days

David's programme began in December of 1998. As with the other families in the text, the family were starting a programme whilst negotiating with the education authority for what they considered to be appropriate provision on David's statement of special educational need. Consequently, the programme began with three tutors, with Ruth and Ben acting as tutors on weekends. The usual beginning programmes were introduced to David and, as outlined below, he made excellent progress with these. David has worked very hard through his programme, the 'learning week' building up to 35 hours very quickly. David's reaction to the programme was, initially, one of some distress at being asked to comply with requests from adults. Asking David to sit on a chair caused major tantrums at first, although once he realised that he would have fun when co-operating with adults, he became much less resistant to requests from others. He soon adopted the routine of snacks, lots of play and lots of fun and relished the structure the programme offered.

Communication

David made outstanding progress in the early part of his programme. After only four months of intervention, he had learned the names of over 50 things in his environment and was able to differentiate the language used in simple requests. He moved from a vocabulary of about five words, used singly, to joining in with nursery rhymes, using greetings, and was able to make a request 'I want…' in response to a question.

Play

Pre-intervention, David's play had consisted mostly of self-stimulatory activities, and this proved a more challenging area for him. However, a psychology report from this time comments on David's developing interest in books, copying brick play and skill with jigsaw puzzles. He was beginning some imitative imaginative play by this time although this was not, as yet, spontaneous play. He continued to enjoy gross motor activities, such as the swings and slide, and his running behaviour changed to bunny-hopping at around this time.

Socialisation

David continued to attend nursery part time through his home learning programme. Almost as soon as the programme started, the nursery staff commented very positively on the change in his behaviour and demeanour. Of particular note was the improvement in his ability to co-operate with requests and how his enhanced communication made playing and working with David so much easier and more rewarding for both him and the nursery staff. His attitude to the other children changed also – he became less aggressive but was still not motivated to play with them.

Behaviour

A consistent approach to David's more challenging behaviour during the first few months of the programme worked very well. Tantrums were treated with extinction – that is, the tantrumming behaviour is ignored, but the child is not. Anyone who has tried to work with a very cross child will appreciate just how difficult this can be but any deviation from the approach can lead to an extension of the tantrumming behaviour. David's team managed this very well and the tantrums started to diminish very quickly. Similarly, his self-stimulatory behaviour was approached through redirecting him to a more appropriate activity and then rewarding him for engaging in it. Again, the nursery staff and other professionals who visited David commented on how much calmer he was after only a few months of intervention.

By the end of his first year of home education, David was transferring skills well into the nursery setting. He was able to make requests for favourite activities, to ask for help, and to follow basic instructions along with the other children. At this stage, the nursery staff also witnessed a decrease in tantrums and running around and an increase in more purposive activity. However, he still had a very low tolerance for other children, particularly if they had toys that he wanted. He was not interested in playing with the others at this point and, although he enjoyed nursery, was rather isolated within the social environment.

Early programming

The beginning of 2000 brought the long-awaited tribunal to settle the question of appropriate intervention for David. One of the things that stands out very clearly for Ruth from these early stages of David's education is the additional worry and work caused by the whole statementing/appeal process which places an enormous burden on family members. Ruth recalls writing many reports for many different agencies over this period – one which took from 3 pm one day to 3 am the next! At this time, Ben was working one to one with David at the weekends in addition to working at his full-time job. However, at the hearing, it was decided that Lovaas intervention was appropriate for David and the programme was then partly funded by the education authority. This resulted in a huge financial burden on the family being significantly reduced, which in turn reduced a great deal of stress. David's home education has been managed throughout by his mother, who brought skills in person management from the workplace to apply to the establishment and maintenance of the team of people, at home and at school, who have been responsible for David's education. This is a huge undertaking which Ruth has accomplished with efficiency, grace and humour.

Communication

By March 2000, David's communication and language skills were expanding rapidly. At this point, work was focused on the use of pronouns and on asking questions appropriately (e.g. asking a range of 'wh' questions rather than relying on 'what?'). David's home teaching team was also helping him to use richer language, including the adjectives he knew, into his everyday communication. As is typical of him, David used his language skills very adequately for requesting desired objects or activities, but not in a social fashion.

Towards the end of the year, some more complex issues were broached. For example, David began to learn the difference between 'asking' and 'telling'. Another step forward was learning when and how to use 'I don't know'. I am sure that parents often wish their children didn't know this phrase as it can become a default response, covering 'I can't be bothered' as well as its actual meaning! The past tense was also introduced at this stage – David was asked do something (e.g. go to another room) and then asked about the activity, prompting a natural use of the past tense. Given that David was pre-verbal at the beginning of his programme, this was phenomenal progress.

Socialisation and play

Play dates had become an important part of David's programme, enabling him to practise his burgeoning social skills in a structured environment. At this stage, three play dates per week were organised for David, each lasting for about 45 minutes. Within this time, the tutor would organise a craft activity (which David really enjoyed), a turn-taking game, some singing, a snack and a story time. This high level of structure was necessary, as, in a less structured environment, David was likely to abandon his play pal and begin to read or to engage in self-stimulatory bed jumping. The play dates were not a favourite part of David's week at this point in his education, but his parents persevered with the provision of opportunities to rehearse social skills.

David was also attending nursery more frequently at this point and from April of 2000 had three mornings a week with the other children. Whilst the programme had certainly enabled David's participation in the nursery environment, he remained rather uninterested in the other children, preferring to play alone when the opportunity arose. Structured play with other children was not problematic and he would always join in as asked but would, by choice, be alone.

In moving David's play along developmentally (Sheridan, Harding and Meldon-Smith 1999), his team introduced some play involving the use of imagination. Initially, this was at the 'Let's pretend…' level (e.g. 'Let's pretend we're cats') in order to introduce the whole concept of pretending. This can be problematic for children on the autistic spectrum, who can be very literal in their understanding of the world (Whitman 2004) and so it is important to build up this ability in very small steps. Once David was able to respond to and generate suggestions for pretending, the team introduced some symbolic play – pretending that one object is something else. David did well with this, and was able to generate short sequences of pretend play by the end of the year. Incidentally, this is where the title of David's chapter comes from: having grasped the idea of dressing up and pretending, David had a 'Woody' suit which he wore for a few days, declaring, 'I'm not David, I'm Woody'. Ruth comments that this strand of David's programme has caused more difficulty for his tutors than any other. Whilst the work at the table is fairly tightly pre-scribed, the play elements of the programme demand that adults be able and comfortable to play alongside and with a child. This is not a gift possessed by many adults and pretend play particularly can be stilted or forced – an attitude that transmits itself to the child quickly. Ruth had to work hard throughout the programme to seek out and recruit tutors who were talented, able and, above all, lots of fun to ensure that play was appealing to David.

Behaviour

Despite making good progress through 2000, David experienced some diffi-culties with behaviour during this period. Early in the year, the tantrums, which had faded away, began to reappear, this time with more shouting. His team responded by teaching him more appropriate ways of expressing his emotion and focused on rewarding appropriate behaviours much more heavily than previously. A little later in the year, this evolved into a token economy system, as David was able to deal with delayed reinforcement. Ruth and Ben feel that periods of challenging behaviour from David usually coincide with ill health, connected to his on-going gastrointestinal difficulties. While recognising that there may be a physiological basis for David's behaviour, they feel that, in order to help him through these periods, consistency of expectation is crucial. Thus, undesirable behaviours were managed to the same behavioural guidelines regardless of cause, thus avoiding confusion for David about behavioural boundaries.

Pre-academics

As David was due to transfer to the local primary school in August 2000, his home education team began some pre-academic work with him. For the child on the autistic spectrum, coping with the language and social demands of school can be a full-time task in itself (Attwood 1998) and so it is often helpful to prepare the child for the academic challenges that will be presented. Through the year, David learned to copy letters and to write his name free hand. He also began to do some drawing of objects. Towards the end of the year, his teacher at school and team at home focused on David's pencil grip and the size and formation of letters. The dyspraxia which is so commonly a part of individuals' autism (Blakemore-Brown 2002) causes major problems for many children in learning to write. Indeed, even after having mastered the skill of forming letters, the questions of placement, size and orientation continue to be troubling for many. David is starting to learn to use a keyboard in order to remove the pressure on writing as his major form of output at school.

David also began some numeracy work in preparation for school and by June 2000 was able to write numbers up to ten and count up to 20, with one-to-one correspondence. Reading was another focus for this strand of the curriculum, and David moved from sight-reading to using the Oxford Reading Tree (ORT) scheme (see References) which aided his understanding enormously. Again with school preparation in mind, Ruth and the team encouraged David to work at tasks independently. Closed-end tasks were prepared for him and he worked at a small number of these, with minimal prompting.

Measuring progress

The enormous progress made by David has been apparent and a source of delight to his family and team throughout the programme. However, in order to give an objective measure of progress, he has had a battery of tests of cognitive, language and social ability on an annual basis. (This is, indeed, the case for all of the children who appear in this book, with the exception of John.) David has always presented an interesting clinical picture; he presents with profound autism and a high IQ. The tests have reflected an increase in performance each year, most notably in the early years of the programme. David's profile at the beginning of his home education was an extreme of that which one might anticipate for a child on the autistic spectrum: he scored significantly below his age level on language and social skills but way above it in terms of non-verbal IQ. Indeed, he ranged well into the adult level of performance on some of the non-verbal tests, causing the tester some difficulty in keeping ahead! The profile has evened out to some extent over the years of intervention, given the increase in David's linguistic, reasoning and social skills, but continues to reflect the strengths David has in the realm of visual-spatial skills.

Mid-programming

Throughout 2001 David's team settled into the huge task of teaching him the vast range of abilities and information that typically developing children acquire incidentally, as well as extending his range of more naturalistic learning skills. This year also marked the move to Year 1 at school, a change which poses tremendous challenges for children on the autistic spectrum. The expectations of children increase enormously through the first years at primary school, and school changes from a free-flowing, play-based environment to one much more concerned with targets and assessments (Wragg 2001). For children who find the practicalities of school (sitting still, managing pencils, interacting, processing language) difficult, the increased expectation can lead to a loss of confidence and ability to use the skills they have.

Communication

David had reached quite a sophisticated level of communication, learning to use pronouns, asking 'what', 'where' and 'who' questions and speaking consistently in sentences rather than phrases or single words. However, his limited motivation to engage with others began to fall off during 2001, and David needed a revision of some of the earlier strategies to encourage appropriate social communication. His team was also working on naturalising his language, introducing more flexibility into his speech. For example, a range of phrases that children might typically use when playing was taught to David, and he was encouraged to use these at school and during his play dates.

Socialisation and play

David's parents persevered with arranging play dates after school hours for him, despite the fact that he still was not particularly motivated by the presence of other children. He had a good range of play skills by this stage, but was still at the stage of playing alongside rather than with other children, unless in a very structured environment.

One area of socialisation that requires attention in most children on the autistic spectrum is that of emotional understanding (Whitman 2004). This is a vast topic, presenting ground to be covered with the child in the realms of both theory and practice. For many things we teach children, there is a clear external referent: that is, if we want to teach the child (for example) the word 'cup', we can point to first one cup, then many different types of cup in order to teach the concept of 'open drinking vessel, usually with a handle'. However, emotions are internal feelings and the only referent we have for understanding is the person's behaviour and a cognitive appraisal of the circumstances in which the emotional behaviour is displayed. Given the difficulties children on the autistic spectrum have with 'other minds' (Baron-Cohen, Leslie and Frith 1985) and that difficulty with interpreting social situations is by definition problematic, it is not surprising that this field presents so many challenges. The child on the autistic spectrum may need to work from a very basic level of understanding what particular facial expressions mean (Howlin, Baron-Cohen and Hadwin 1998), move to understanding that events cause emotions and thus to being able to predict an emotional response to a given situation (e.g. the little girl's picture has fallen into a puddle – how will she feel?). The Howlin, Baron-Cohen and Hadwin text (1998) takes this teaching through four levels of increasing sophistication in understanding others' emotions, but a further difficulty often lies in the child's ability to understand their own emotions. Often, teaching needs to be just as overt in this field, and appropriate behaviour must be explained and rehearsed in different circumstances (Smith Myles and Southwick 1999).

At this point, David was still very intolerant of other children, and was not comfortable with the flexibility of interaction and play. His team spent quite some time targeting his ability to share and to negotiate with other children, and David has found this easier over the past few years.

Behaviour

Again, during this period, we faced the rather odd situation where David was learning at a fast pace, and yet he and his team were suffering from his rather challenging behaviour. A cost-response system was introduced at the height of this episode, where David would lose stars from his board should undesirable behaviours appear. He could earn these back, and his reward was two cups of blueberries (a firm favourite). Even with the loss of some stars, one cup of blueberries would be forthcoming, but the extra cup proved a sufficient incentive for much more appropriate behaviours.

Academics

By this stage of the programme, David's school attendance had increased to four mornings per week and he was receiving 20 hours' learning at home. It is at this stage in a home programme where the balance between the academic support given at home and school targets needs to be finely set. Clearly, one would support the child at home by addressing any issues that were of concern in the classroom, but the child's academic education is, rightly, the school's remit. Thus, David was given the opportunity to rehearse academic skills at home, but this work followed the school's curriculum.

Later programming

David's home education programme lasted rather longer than a typical Lovaas programme. One of the aims of the intervention is to move the child away from discrete trial teaching and toward more naturalistic means of learning in preparation for full-time school placement. However, David continued to make good progress with this style and so continued to learn in this way at home alongside more traditional learning in school. By mid-2002, David was spending from 9 am to 2 pm in school, Monday to Thursday, the remainder of his learning week being spent in one-to-one work. He also continued with his play curriculum. Tony Attwood (1998) suggests that full-time school can prove too much of a strain for children on the autistic spectrum and that part-time school and regular breaks from school might be necessary to maintain the individual child's physical, psychological and emotional equilibrium. The educational week outlined above allows him to follow the school curriculum adequately and provides time to address the difficulties he has relating to his autism.

Through this final phase of David's programme, the emphasis was on pushing further forward the skills he had already gained. For example, in liaison with the speech and language therapist, quite some time was spent on logical reasoning work – having David think through scenarios and pictures and draw inferences from and reason about the stories told. Work also focused on having David both understand and use more expanded language, rather than the somewhat telegraphic style that is clearly easier for him to use.

As one would anticipate, the work became less discrete-trial based and took on more of a feel of a programme designed to meet social, cognitive and language needs. One example of this is the use of a 'circle of friends' approach to appropriate interaction with other people. David identified those people important to him and the range of interpersonal behaviours that it is appropriate to engage in with each of these people. I have seen similar exercises done as part of more eclectic home education and also in social skills groups in schools (Aarons and Gittens 2001).

In the realm of play, David's interest in the theatre has boosted his ability to use his imagination. He enjoys the puppet theatre and initially worked to scripted stories. More recently, he has demonstrated the ability to be more spontaneous with this, when a story line is introduced. David continued to have friends to his home to play during the week, which now both he and the friends enjoy. It gives them the opportunity to do things that the National Curriculum has squeezed out of the school day, but which children might not necessarily do at home, for example, playing board games or engaging in craft activities. Whilst David no longer follows a Lovaas curriculum, he continues to learn at home, in a manner appropriate to his age. Particular issues relating to his autism can be addressed thoroughly and he can expand socially through attending the art club, theatre club and swimming.

In conclusion

Ruth feels that using applied behavioural analysis has brought consistent improvement in David's abilities over his early childhood. She is convinced that the programme has enabled him to attend mainstream school and above all, that he is more happy, settled and fulfilled than he ever could have been without it. The programme has formed the basis of everything she and Ben have done for David, forming a solid bedrock of learning on which to build. It has also equipped them both with confidence, skills and effective strategies to go on helping David overcome his difficulties and enjoy life. Establishing and maintaining the programme, ensuring competent and reliable tutors were available and generalising David's learning were very hard work for the intensive part of his learning at home. Ruth is glad to have had such good liaison with David's school via the shadows and enthusiastic teachers, as this has made keeping David's education on track considerably easier.

David has had a marvellous school placement through his primary and junior years and this chapter ends with a reflection by the deputy head of the infant section of the school who was also David's class teacher for a year, on her experiences of having a 'Lovaas child' in school.

A teacher's perspective

Getting to know David

I like to think of myself as up for any challenge, and being a teacher certainly enables this to be fulfilled regularly!

The head of the school at the time asked about having a child with autism in my class, and my immediate reaction was, 'Great, a new challenge ahead and another dimension to add to my teaching'. Not really being sure about what autism was or what that would mean I had no hesitation in saying yes. After all, all children have something they can teach us!

I then learned that the little boy who was going to start in the class was not having support from the LEA but rather from a Lovaas programme. To be honest that didn't really mean that much to me initially but when I learned more about what support he was getting, my reactions were two-fold. First – wow! – what a great impact this must be having on him as it was so intense, and how each step had been so carefully broken down; but then – poor child – to be continually having to be taught concepts that we take for granted must be incredibly tiring.

David came to visit me in class, and the whole-learning concepts which he still needed to learn became apparent. He headed straight for the computer when he came in, evidently something he could identify with, although 'Nursery Rhyme Time' was too exciting and he literally jumped up and down in front of the computer while it was playing.

My teaching assistant at the time and I went to visit David at his home to gain a deeper insight into what he could do and to understand what the Lovaas programme was helping David to achieve. We observed him play on the computer and be taught a new concept in his bedroom, a place where he felt safe and also where he had a time-out place to go – which was in fact jumping on his bed!!! We observed the repetition of the activity and of the need to ensure that we had David's full attention. We learned of the need to break steps down into smaller, more manageable chunks, and of the need to keep revisiting to ensure that concepts had been learnt.

My photo was taken so that David could learn who I was before he started. It was a weird feeling to be compartmentalised. I had never really thought of myself as having to be learnt.

While being on the home visit we also learned about David's eating habits and how he was on a gluten-free diet. This meant that whenever we did cooking in school I was able to tell his mum and she never failed in finding a match for what David could eat and what we were going to be cooking that week.

Starting school

When David started in the September he first taught me the importance of a routine and how important it is to warn all children of any changes. We had a fire alarm practice within the first few weeks. Fortunately I had had the foresight to warn David's mother, as I didn't know how he would react to a loud noise. Most children in the class are frightened by a loud noise. David taught me how much I can talk and when enough is enough! If there was too much language for David he would suddenly start singing nursery rhymes. At first I thought, that was just David, but then I realised he was trying to tell me something. It was a good wake up call!

David needed to sit near the back of the group so when he needed a break it was easier for him to move. We gave him a mat to sit on to start with. The rest of the children soon realised that was David's place. One child in my class at the time described David's condition to another child by saying 'David's brain doesn't work like ours' – a simple but very factual comment.

David taught me how important it is to have differing teaching styles and the importance of visual aids – thank goodness for laminators, a PC and a scanner! Visual timetables are a must and I now use them with all the children with whom I work! David started school with a 'shadow'; the word used for his support I have never approved of but the assistance that he received was unquestionable. The shadow had a great strength in being able to fit easily into the working environment, quickly seeing what needed to be done and helped in finding manageable ways of achieving these goals for David, and also in training me in supporting him. We had one member of staff who had no idea of how to treat David and cornered him one lunchtime because of the 'unknown'. This led me to realise that we must never assume that everybody can support children and that if we are to take on new challenges we have to be prepared to listen, learn, talk about our anxieties and then work out strategies for ourselves to overcome these eventualities. The smallest concepts to us can be massive hurdles for some children.

The shadow had a very clear and deep understanding of the needs of an autistic child. She was able to convey the strategies that we would need to use to help him to not only the reception team, but also to other adults who had contact with David. Initially the Lovaas and school curriculum had different expectations. This was frustrating for me as I wanted David to be learning about the concepts he was doing in school. However, because of the shadow's good communication, planning, regular meetings, constant reviews and setting of targets within school both needs could be met. She was always updating her notes and records, and ensured that the school had copies of everything she did. I went along to a planning meeting with the Lovaas programme and was able to put across the concepts that I felt were important for David to be learning. These ideas were then combined with the programme he was receiving at home as well. It is no good just being able to improve on number skills when other basic concepts need working on as well. I now realise that often if you are secure in doing something you are willing to do more of it, but if something is hard you tend to give up because you haven't got the confidence in yourself to do more of it – how important it is to continually be raising self-esteem.

Progress

I quote from a report I wrote about David's first term at school with us:

> David started school in September and initially attended for three mornings a week; this has now been increased to four and since Christmas four mornings and one afternoon. David has made progress in certain areas in school, but his limited ability to relate to other children is still an area that needs a continued focus. David knows the names of several of the children in the class, and always gets 'Sam' or 'two Sams' right, but often tends to call the girls 'Rebecca'. With a quick reminder he will guess again and sometimes with the initial sounds as a clue he will get it right.
>
> It is great to hear David talking more in school. He can make himself understood more easily and is beginning to make some responses to either myself or to other children, often by repeating what he has just heard. He has even started testing his shadow!

David has learned the school routine and although he needs to be reminded he will follow the daily routine quite well. His obsession with the computer first thing in the morning has dwindled, although he will always choose to play with it wherever possible. He is happy to use different programmes now rather than just 'Nursery Rhyme Time'!

David started school ahead of the other children with his reading, but he could not recognise many of the reception key words. He has mastered most of these now and is working his way through the ORT scheme well; he has now just begun to learn to spell these words. There are many children in the class who are of David's level.

David knows most of his letters and sounds. He needs lots of encouragement. His writing is beginning to be phonetic but it is quite clear what he has written e.g. 'thu' for 'the'. He has begun to write single sentences. Lots of the other children are managing this unaided. However, David has been placed in the top group this term to encourage him to use other children as role models.

David understands simple mathematical concepts, but the mathematical language is often confusing for him. The Lovaas staff have a copy of what we are covering each week in school so that things can be taught to David ahead of meeting it in school. David finds the language of number fans very confusing and is often easily distracted. He needs lots of one to one here.

David showed me even more clearly me how important the needs of individual children are and how important it is to use many different teaching styles – visual and auditory as well as kinaesthetic. He taught me of the need to ensure that the language we use is obvious and clear. He showed me the need to keep instructions to a minimum but to the point. He showed me that we need to always remember where the child is starting from and that we all start from many different places, and to find the concept or idea that encourages and motivates, whether it be cars, Noddy or churches!

References

Aarons, M. and Gittens, T. (2001) *Autism: A Social Skills Approach for Children and Adolescents.* Bicester: Speechmark Publishing Ltd.

Attwood, T. (1998) *Asperger's Syndrome: A Guide for Parents and Professionals.* London: Jessica Kingsley Publishers.

Baron-Cohen, S., Leslie, A. and Frith, U. (1985) 'Does the autistic child have a "Theory of Mind"?' *Cognition,* 21, 37–46.

Blakemore-Brown, L. (2002) *Reweaving the Autistic Tapestry: Autism, Asperger Syndrome and ADHD.* London: Jessica Kingsley Publishers.

Buttar, R. (2004) 'Autism, the Misdiagnosis of our Future Generations.' US Congressional Sub-Committee Hearing, 6 May. Available at www.generationrescue.org/pdf/news/buttar.pdf (accessed 8 December 2006).

Holmes, A., Baxill, M. and Haley, B. (2003) 'Reduced levels of mercury in first baby haircuts of autistic children.' *International Journal of Toxicology*, 22 (4), 277–285.

Howlin, P., Baron-Cohen, S. and Hadwin, J. (1998) *Teaching Children with Autism to Mind Read.* Chichester: John Wiley and Sons Ltd.

Jordan, R., Jones, G. and Murray, D. (1998) *Educational Interventions for Children with Autism: A Literature Review of Recent and Current Research.* London: DfEE.

Le Breton, M. (2001) *Diet Intervention and Autism: Implementing the Gluten Free and Casein Free Diet for Autistic Children and Adults – A Practical Guide for Parents.* London: Jessica Kingsley Publishers.

McCandless, J., Binstock, T. and Zimmerman, J. (2003) *Children with Starving Brains: A Medical Treatment Guide for Autistic Spectrum Disorder.* London: Bramble Books.

Oxford Reading Tree scheme. www.oup.com/oxed/primary/literacy/ort (accessed 8 December 2006).

Sheridan, M., Harding, J. and Meldon-Smith, L. (1999) *Play in Early Childhood: From Birth to Six Years.* London: Routledge.

Smith Myles, B. and Southwick, J. (1999) *Asperger Syndrome and Difficult Moments: Practical Solutions for Tantrums, Rage, and Meltdowns.* Shawnee Mission, KS: Asperger Publishing Co.

Whitman, T. (2004) *The Development of Autism: A Self-Regulatory Perspective.* London: Jessica Kingsley Publishers.

Wragg, E. (2001) *Assessment and Children's Learning in the Primary School.* London: RoutledgeFalmer.

Chapter 6

Oli's Tale

Tip That Spoon

Oli is a delightful boy who is now seven years old. He looks angelic – he has curly blond hair, gorgeous eyes and a remarkably cheeky grin, which gives a hint to his mischievous nature. Oli lives in rural Norfolk and is the middle child of three. His older sister, Francesca, is a lovely girl, who is keen on dancing. Oli's younger brother, Ruben, is a lively toddler, bright and interested in everything.

Oli is a very active little chap. He is almost constantly on the move and enjoys being outside. His favourite activity is playing on swings and climbing frames. He is an engaging and affectionate child who will greet others appropriately and spontaneously hugs and kisses people he knows and likes. Yet as well as autism, Oli has some very complex needs. He has additional learning difficulties that have become apparent over the course of his home and school education. Oli's epilepsy also constitutes a challenge to his physical well-being and his ability to learn. In common with many other children on the autistic spectrum, Oli suffers quite badly with very poor digestion and this can cause him considerable pain and discomfort. Despite this, Oli is generally a busy and happy boy, who is great fun.

Pre-intervention

Oli's infancy was, unfortunately, marked by a series of illnesses – he was troubled with ear infections and colds and at the age of ten months contracted viral meningitis. Subsequently, Oli developed epilepsy and this has been controlled with medication over the years, with varying degrees of success. His family was offered early intervention by the local education authority, which ran a Portage (Burke and Cigno 2000) scheme at that time. Philippa and Simon (Oli's parents) felt that this was not sufficiently intensive to make any real difference to Oli's learning and, after extensive research, chose to begin a Lovaas programme.

When I first met Oli, the two most obvious things about him were that he was never still and that he drank constantly. He carried a cup with a feeder top around with him and drank many litres of diluted juice through the course of the day. It was really very difficult to engage Oli at this time – he avoided contact very actively and responded little to verbal or physical cues in his environment. He would, however, kiss people, although at this time his affection was indiscriminate. Oli did not have a communication system and would pull people toward whatever he wanted. Just as the programme began, Philippa had started work on teaching Oli to point. When frustrated, Oli would tantrum quite spectacularly and, at this time, had some pervasive self-stimulatory behaviours. These were mostly visual, although he did have some fairly archetypal hand-flapping.

Oli as a toddler

Beginning Oli's programme

Oli's family, like the other families in this book, began his programme whilst going through the process of negotiation with the local education authority to gain funding for home education. In Oli's case, this was rather protracted and ended with the local education authority offering part-funding a matter of days before the date set for the Special Educational Needs Tribunal. Prior to this, Oli's teaching team had consisted of his parents, his paternal grandmother and a delightful young woman who had previously worked with the family. On receipt of funding, the team expanded quite rapidly to consist of four tutors, Oli's mum and his grandmother.

Mum on the far right, Grandma on the far left, Oli on everyone's lap!

The discussions I have had with other home educators reflect mixed feelings with regard to having family members acting as tutors. Given the funding situation, this is sometimes inevitable: some family members recognise the importance of adopting a different role for their 'tutor' time; others find this very difficult and mix emotional and educational responses. In this case, Philippa managed Oli's programme with enormous expertise and was a tough task master for Oli. His grandmother worked ably and consistently with Oli for the duration of his intensive programme and provided a stable base for his learning.

Early programming

During the first few months of Oli's programme, the initial items from the Lovaas curriculum were introduced: non-verbal imitation, receptive instructions, puzzles, matching (Leaf and McEachin 1999). As always, play was a huge part of Oli's 'working day'. Initially, he could stay at the table for only very short periods of time and so free and guided play were a major part of his learning. Finding a range of reinforcers for Oli proved challenging at first. While he was happy to receive social reinforcement, we felt, given the vast amount of work ahead of him, that this might pall over time, particularly as the demands of the programme increased. Thus a range of toy reinforcers was paired with the social reinforcement, which not only gave variety but also helped to increase Oli's interest in toys.

Oli's programme began in April 2000: by Christmas, he was acquiring skills at a good pace. Most pleasingly, he had a range of toy-play skills that he could use at nursery, which he attended for two sessions a week. Learning to respond to a request to wait (essential at any nursery!) was challenging for Oli but he did learn this and was able to comply most of the time.

Also during this first year, the team enabled Oli to use the toilet appropriately. Only a few months were needed to acquire this skill and by Christmas he was able to recognise and respond to his need to use the toilet. He was probably aided in this learning by the amount he was drinking, as he had plenty of opportunity for practice. This was still quite a pervasive behaviour outside his learning sessions, but we had faded out the drinking in his play/work room, again, by Christmas. This was accomplished in very small steps, enabling Oli to put his cup down and gradually increasing the periods of time between drinks.

Oli attended the local nursery class during the early part of his programme and one of his home tutors accompanied him to help him make the most of the learning opportunities available. The nursery staff were very positive about Oli's attendance and keen to learn about his home programme. The presence of an adult on a one-to-one basis with a child can be challenging for nursery or school staff. My experience would suggest that if the child presents with complex learning and behavioural needs, the temptation is to allow the additional adult to take a larger role than is necessarily optimal for the child's education. The inclusion of children with complex needs in mainstream settings raises a whole new agenda for schools and for individual teachers (Jones 2004, Thomas and Vaughan 2004). While most teachers are hugely skilled and flexible in their practice, the levels of expertise required by some children calls for additional educational input for the school and individual teachers. This requires not just blanket sessions on the kinds of difficulties teachers might come across (e.g. a couple of days on autism or attentional problems) but detailed specialist work with individual children in the classroom.

Mid-programming

The Christmas holidays in 2000 were the first break Oli had had from his home programme and his behaviour deteriorated quite markedly over this period. At the same time, there was an increase in his seizure activity. Careful assessment on the part of the team revealed that Oli's appearance of aggression (hitting and grabbing) and the decrease in his ability to focus preceded a seizure, and that both behaviours were ameliorated by the seizure. Oli's paediatrician at this time was manipulating his medication to find the optimal dosage and timing. We acknowledged the physiological trigger for the

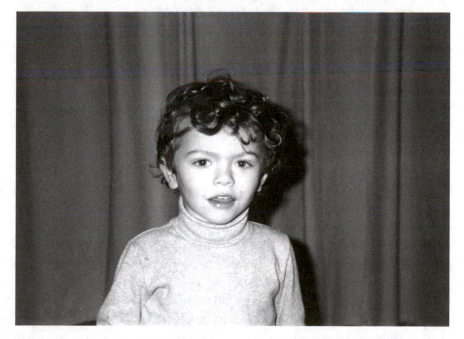

Growing up

behaviours, and responded with an ignore-redirect approach (McBrien and Felce 1995), while carefully monitoring the behavioural and seizure changes.

Despite these difficulties, Oli continued to make good progress through 2001.

Communication

During this year, Oli expanded his receptive vocabulary enormously. He learned the names of more than a hundred everyday items and was able to generalise this knowledge very quickly. Oli also learned to respond appropriately to a large number of requests, differentiating the language used very well. The data here are sometimes a little wobbly as Oli might sometimes choose not to do as he was asked, despite having previously shown us that he understood the request. Non-cued items (those with no visual clue) were more challenging for him and his team learned the importance of bolstering Oli's confidence adequately when he was learning new items.

In relation to icon use, a visual timetable was used at nursery and at home for much of this year (Krantz, MacDuff and McClannahan 1993), but Oli continued to require prompting to use it. At first, we thought that he was not connecting the icon to the pictured activity and addressed this using a variety of teaching approaches. However, even after this, the timetable held no interest for Oli. In retrospect, I feel this may have been because Oli had little sense of time. He was not a child who did things according to an internal clock (meal or break times, for example) and so the chunking of time may not have had any meaning for him at this stage in his development.

Play and socialisation

Throughout 2001, Oli's team worked on his ability to play independently (i.e. without adult support) and to play with other children. Prior to this work Oli could play with toys with support but his 'default' pastime was self-stimulatory behaviour. Much effort was expended in teaching Oli to use the play skills he had more widely. Oli's interest in other children had waxed and waned through his early childhood. Sometimes over the years he has really surprised us: on one occasion, the children leaving nursery had a game of rolling down the grass bank. Oli joined in. More recently, his siblings were playing in the garden next door. Oli had a peep over the fence and when asked if he wanted to play too, replied, 'yeah' and went round for a few minutes. By the end of 2001 Oli was showing a passing interest in other children at nursery. He would not approach them for interaction but had no objection to working in the same place as them and co-operating in activities such as assembling jigsaws and painting. While he is clearly fond of his siblings, Oli has never made a 'special friend' at nursery or school and I feel this is reflective of his level of interest in others rather than his ability to play.

Later programming

Throughout the following year (2002) Oli continued to learn at a steady pace, although he was not acquiring concepts at his previous rate. It was becoming apparent that, in terms of his cognitive abilities, we were reaching a ceiling for Oli for this stage of his development. For example, Oli struggled greatly with the concept of functions and, although he gained a few items, his family and team felt that the effort expended here could be better spent on teaching more immediately useful skills.

Oli's birthday, with Francesca and Ruben

Communication

By this stage, Oli was using his PECS very successfully. He could find his book (wherever he had left it), form a sentence and point out the parts of the sentence to whoever he was 'talking' to. Oli used PECS mainly to ask for things, but has occasionally spontaneously used the system for social communication. He learned to use icons indicating colour expressively and also some action labels.

Oli had begun to use his voice more through this year and so we began some work on enabling him to use his voice communicatively. He had always been a great hummer and we started to enable him to gain some further control over this vocalisation. We paired movements with sounds and encouraged Oli to copy them. He did amazingly well with this and consequently learned to copy speech sounds. Eventually this work has enabled him to form a few words (e.g. yes, no, yoghurt, drink) which he uses reliably. Although this work is presented in a couple of sentences, those familiar with helping children acquire these skills will appreciate that this developed over the course of many months' teaching (Kolberg 2004).

For Oli, the process of learning to use 'yes' and 'no' was a long haul. Initially he was taught to nod and shake his head through imitation as Oli did not have these as part of his natural gesture repertoire. He was then taught to respond to the question, 'Do you want this?' which initially required full modelling of the appropriate response but he gained the skill within a few months. By August, Oli was indicating 'no' reliably and both 'yes' and 'no' by October. This was very useful for him and a later step in this process was to pair the gestures with the words in order to teach Oli to say both 'yes' and 'no' which he does beautifully.

As part of Oli's listening skills, he also worked on recognising sounds in his environment. Previously, he did not react to the door bell or telephone, but after some painstaking discrete trial work, he now knows the appropriate response to these sounds. He will, in fact, fetch the telephone for his mum if she's busy when it rings.

Play and socialisation

With his burgeoning language ability, we introduced some symbolic play to Oli's play programme. He had a very lovely farm set and, as he knew animal sounds, we spent some time playing with that. We also set up play scenarios from the real-life activities he enjoyed – travelling in the car, going to the park. Oli was entirely unimpressed by even our best efforts. At this time, he was most interested in playing a board game which involved hooking small monkeys together and our attempts to engage him with the farm were not nearly so interesting.

We also continued to promote Oli's ability to play independently through using play stations in his play room, at first, and then in the rest of the house (Leaf and McEachin 1999). This was a successful strategy for some of the time. Oli does not have difficulty in entertaining himself: however, his choice of activities would involve a high degree of physical activity and not inconsiderable proportion of self-stimulatory behaviour. Thus, it was important to continue to prompt Oli to use his spare time more constructively.

Oli received invitations to a few birthday parties from his peers at school. This was a lovely opportunity for Oli to see the children in different circumstances and he did seem to enjoy the events. He also had some play dates, where children from school came home to play with him. These, however, were not easily arranged and Oli's family and team felt that his motivation was not really high enough to persevere with these arrangements.

Behaviour

As the earlier sections of this chapter have indicated, through his childhood thus far, Oli had some periods of time where his behaviour became quite challenging. Throughout all of these, his team and family have shown an excellent understanding of the importance of consistent management (McCue 2000) along with a rare sensitivity to Oli's needs. Meticulous records have been kept of Oli's aggressive incidents, along with more qualitative data on his mood, level of attention and engagement. This has been invaluable in many ways. First, an accurate assessment of the causes and triggers for Oli's aggression enables appropriate intervention to be planned (Reed and Head 1993). For example, the team members were able to distinguish between 'before-seizure' agitation and purposive aggression by taking careful note of its form, frequency and so on (McConnell, Hilvitz and Cox 1998). Second, as anyone who engages with a child who has periods of aggression will know, these can be emotionally devastating for the family and adults working with the child. During these periods, feelings of hopelessness and helplessness are common: good record-keeping gives indicators of successful previous intervention and the knowledge that this, too, will pass (Smith Myles and Southwick 1999). Finally, a behavioural approach to aggressive/destructive/self-injurious behaviour gives a pattern to which to adhere during very difficult times. It is empowering to know that there is a plan and that it will help the child.

Oli has been very fortunate in being surrounded by a loving family and caring tutors who have been able to support him through difficult times. I would not suggest that having a supportive team and strong behavioural strategies makes managing the periods easy – these things do, however, help to make them more bearable.

School

At Oli's review in 2002 it was felt that it would be beneficial for Oli to spend some of his week at a local school for children with special educational needs. However, although Philippa and Simon recognised that Oli had needs additional to his autism and that the special school has staff and resources appropriate for these needs, they were keen for Oli to retain some contact with the local children. Thus, when Oli returned to school in September, he had rather a mixed week: some local school attendance, some special school attendance, some learning at home. This meant a very full week for Oli, but he absolutely thrived on all the stimulation.

Clearly, as Oli's school hours increased so the range of material targeted at home decreased. I feel this may well have coincided with a point where we were hitting Oli's academic ceiling. Some quite difficult concepts, such as 'first and last', 'same and different', were the next 'Lovaas' moves in terms of Oli's cognitive curriculum. Despite some fairly drastic programme pruning, so that in the hours available the existing programmes could be addressed frequently, these concepts were clearly rather too challenging for Oli at this stage in his development. Toward the end of 2002, as was appropriate for his age, Oli's school hours increased again and the beginning of 2003 saw his home team having a re-think about the most appropriate use of Oli's home learning time.

Leaving Lovaas

Through 2003 and into 2004 Oli's home learning has gradually undergone a shift from an intensive, discrete-trial teaching approach to a programme designed to support him in school and at home. Self-care skills have played a larger part in his learning; communication and language continue to be a strong focus and play has come more to the centre of the programme again. In this change, we have avoided some common pitfalls that I have witnessed many times in the use of Lovaas intervention in the UK.

One of these pitfalls reflects a lack of communication and planning in the child's education, and the programme ends as a result of the funding for the child's education being targeted on school rather than on the home programme. In this (probably worst possible) scenario, the child has been learning in a particular fashion and rhythm, which ends too abruptly for (everyone's) comfort as school integration has not been planned to accord with the decrease in learning at home. Another pitfall is an increase in the child's school education with little reduction or change to home learning. Thus, the child is expected to learn in two very different ways over the course of a very full week. It would appear obvious that a transitional phase is needed – as one parent put it, 'Even if the funding stops, his autism doesn't.' A shift from a discrete trial approach to more naturalistic ways of teaching should mark the transition period along with the culmination of the assumption of responsibility for the child's education by the school staff. This is not to suggest that parents are in a position to rest on past achievements. As with any child – typically developing or facing some learning disabilities – the ex-Lovaas child may well continue to need help, support and teaching at home. For many children, this teaching will largely reflect their autism – for example, issues of not understanding the difference between teasing and bullying, or the whole question of friendship – and parents may continue to need some expert help on addressing these. However, it is important to recognise that this work is quite distinct from early, intensive intervention – albeit, I am sure, made much easier by it.

Chilling with Dad

And now...

One of the problems raised for parents and practitioners by Lovaas' (1987) original research is the emphasis that has subsequently been placed on the children who, at the end of the programme, are indistinguishable from their peers. I am always delighted when children reach this level of functioning, but this emphasis does rather overshadow the children who make remarkable progress on the programme even if they do not achieve that level. ABA approaches have been used with children and adults with a range of learning difficulties for many decades and we need to acknowledge that success is about the relationship between start and end points of the programme for an individual child rather than measuring that child against some level of 'typicality' (see Buckman 1995).

Opening presents with mum

My expectation is that Oli will remain within the special needs area of UK education through his childhood and adolescence and, as an adult, will require a considerable level of personal support. He is, however, a real star in terms of how much he has learned in his pre- and beginning-school years. Oli has coped with his physical difficulties, his epilepsy, his autism and his additional needs while continuing to learn. Due to the hard work and dedication of his family and tutors, Oli has a vast repertoire of skills and abilities, each one bought dearly in terms of time and effort. These will stand him in good stead for the education that lies ahead of him and I know that he will continue to learn, grow and thrive, cherished by all who know him.

P.S. The title of this chapter is the result of a previous battle of wills, which Oli won hands down. He has a habit when eating – just as he gets his spoon into his mouth, he tips it over and pulls it out of his mouth upside down. This does not pose difficulties when he is eating stodgy foods, but does not work so well with dry or sloppy foods. Consequently, we spent some time encouraging Oli not to tip his spoon over. He can do this very well and we went through a period when Oli would eat 'properly' when anyone was looking at him and revert to his preferred method when not. Given the range of the other difficulties he faces, I came round to Oli's viewpoint in the end so we continue to tip that spoon.

A tutor's perspective

Oliver was extremely fortunate in having, over the years, some highly skilled, motivated and dedicated tutors. Here, Amy Maddison gives her perspective on working with Oli.

I have worked with Oliver for 18 months. Currently I see him for two hours twice a week and I shadow him one day a week in a Year 1 class at a mainstream school. I also work with three other boys on home programmes. Prior to this I had worked with three children on their Lovaas programmes in London, and Oli's was the first family that I met when I moved out to Norfolk. I knew as soon as I met him that I wanted to work with him. He has a very strong personality; he is cheeky, has a great sense of humour and is often affectionate to his tutors. One of the most endearing things about Oliver is that he enjoys humming to himself, and usually has a smile on his face – even if you're not sure what he's smiling about. I often find myself staring at him intently, trying to work out what is going on inside his head. Equally, he may come right up close to my face and stare into my eyes, as if he's trying to work out *me* out. I value the relationship I have with Oli immensely. He has an incredibly infectious laugh, and we frequently get fits of the giggles in session, through tickles, rough and tumble play, chasing, peek-a-boo games, or just the sheer cheek of Oli trying to sneak in some extra stimming when he thinks I won't notice. He can make sessions a lot of fun.

Building a relationship with Oli

Oli can also make sessions very hard work. He was very co-operative when I first started working with him, but after a couple of months his behaviour deteriorated. He started not responding to requests, and found it hard to sit still at the table. He found any prompts to respond to requests hilarious, particularly if they were laced with any emotion he could pick up on. This behaviour was very frustrating as I knew he could be so co-operative, and I had to work hard not to show him I was frustrated. Waiting him out was not practical in short sessions, and in any case if left to his own devices he will quickly find something to stim with. We found that the best strategy was to slowly get up and physically prompt him back to the table, without saying anything or giving him any eye contact. As a team we made more of a fuss of him when he came over straight away. Now we are through that period of non-compliance I very rarely have to prompt him to respond, and can use a natural voice rather than the much sterner voice previously required. It has been very rewarding to build up my relationship with Oli to the point where we know and understand each other, but he does still manage to surprise me and keep me on my toes.

An added complication in my relationship with Oli has been that his moods seem so cyclical. Last summer was very difficult as he became irritable and aggressive, often doling out hard hair-pulls, cheek pinches or attempted bites if he was annoyed. This seems to have been linked to his epilepsy – for a week towards the end of the summer he was having four or five seizures a day, having been seizure-free for a year. So far I have only witnessed one seizure. It was shocking to see all the energy drain out of Oli so quickly. Fortunately Philippa was on hand, particularly so as Oli was at the top of his climbing frame at the time.

Working with the family and team

Philippa has been fantastic to work with, not just when on hand to help rescue a seizure-bound Oli from the top of the climbing frame. She has been deeply involved in the programme since the start, and although she no longer does any actual therapy, she plays a vital part in generalising all we teach Oli in his play room. It is extremely rewarding as a therapist to see a child using their skills every day with his family. Phil has been very supportive of decisions I have made when working at home and at school. I have appreciated greatly the fact that I can always discuss with her any difficulties that have arisen with

Oli, as well as share my excitement with her when he does something wonderful. She has fought for a long time to get the best provision for her son, and it is great to work with someone so motivated. I have always been made to feel very welcome in her home; a cup of tea and a chat with Phil perks me up for my session with Oli, even if I had been feeling exhausted when I arrived. It is important as a therapist that you get on with the child's mother (in my experience it has always been the mother who has been more involved in the programme) as well as with the child. Francesca and Ruben are both delightful and make the house very lively after school – Oli and I sometimes retreat to the sanctuary of his play room to escape the chaos! It has been good to see Fran's friendly face around school when I'm shadowing. Watching Ruben develop naturally skills which Oli is working so hard to learn has been a constant reminder of how amazing child development is. I have not seen very much of Simon as he is usually at work when I'm around but he has been vital in supporting Philippa.

While I have been working with Oli his team have all been young psychology graduates or undergraduates. This team is the only one I work for at present where my colleagues are of a similar age and background to myself, although no one else tutors full time. I have enjoyed working with such like-minded people. It has taken a while to get to know them, which is one of the downsides of such a fragmented job. However, overlaps and workshops have been a lot of fun. We have also had the benefit of excellent supervision from Dr Anderson, who on her visits moves the programme along and makes us all feel very positive about what we are doing.

Learning from Oli

I feel I have learnt a lot from working with Oli. He is the first child I have met who has used PECS as his main method of communication, and as such he is a perfect example of how successful the system can be. Having said that, I have been amazed at how much his verbal ability has developed in the last 18 months. He has mastered seven sounds in Verbal Imitation, has two spoken EOLs (object names) and frequently attempts to imitate play phrases spontaneously. The most fantastic thing has been teaching him to say yes and no – he has mastered these when they are desire-based, which makes offering him something such a natural process, and we are currently teaching him to respond to factual questions. On a couple of occasions Oli has caught someone's eye and strung together several of his speech sounds, as if he's been really trying to say something. I would never have thought when I started working with him that he would develop so much control over his vocalisations, and enjoy this control so much.

Oli's programme has been quite different from any other that I have worked on. He spends most of his week in special school, and so currently receives about ten hours a week of home education, two or three sessions a week after school and all day on Saturdays. I was initially quite concerned about this, wondering how much he would learn with such reduced repetition, and also if he would be too tired after a day at school to work until 6 pm. My worries soon proved to be unfounded. He has made steady progress on his programme, most impressively in the vocal arena, as discussed above. Some programmes have been put on hold as he wasn't making any headway with them, and it is impossible to say whether he would have mastered them if he spent more time in therapy. However, he certainly continues to learn and seems to enjoy the variety that is in his programme. The after-school sessions don't present any difficulties in terms of his energy levels either – in fact we think he appreciates having further structure in what would otherwise be a long afternoon and evening of free time.

I know that the programme has made a huge difference to Oli and his family. Obviously giving him a communication system has greatly improved the quality of his life. Prior to starting on Lovaas all Oli knew how to do was climb. Now he can sit at a table and work for 20 minutes or so at a time, he can express his needs and he has a variety of play skills. His receptive vocabulary is huge, and he can respond appropriately to lengthy instructions delivered in natural language if in context. He has built up different relationships with each of his tutors, and can play appropriately with his brother and sister. He knows what is and what isn't acceptable behaviour. He has very good self-care skills – he was toilet-trained very quickly, can dress himself with minimal prompts and feed himself without any mess. I think he enjoys the structure that sessions add to his day, and enjoys the one-to-one attention, away from what can be quite a busy household. Now Oli is a happy little boy with a high degree of independence and many skills, he is much easier to live with. As one of the other mums that I work for says, 'It's through helping our children that we help ourselves.' Phil knows what strategies to employ if Oli misbehaves out of session. She also values the time that Oli's sessions give her when she knows he is engaged productively and she can spend time with Fran, Ruben and Simon.

Tutoring as a career

I love working with Oli and my other boys. It is a fulfilling job which I fell into by chance, and I'm so pleased I did. Prior to starting work I had had one lecture on autism, and so had a fairly rudimentary understanding of it. Now I find autism absolutely fascinating, read a lot of literature about it and attend conferences when possible, and I still feel I'm only scraping the surface of the condition. It provides a constant intellectual challenge. Tutoring, particularly Lead Tutoring, involves a considerable amount of problem-solving. There is also of course the emotional aspect, the satisfaction of building up relation-ships with these fascinating children, and watching them make progress. It is the most wonderful feeling when you see a child use a skill in real life that you have helped to teach him or her in the work room.

There are also down sides to tutoring full time. The most significant is the pay, which as a graduate I have found appalling. It is what forces many people to leave the profession, and it may well make me try other things. The whole system desperately needs regulating, and recognised pay scales based on skill level should be implemented on a national level. LEAs being short-sighted and refusing to fund programmes mean many parents can't afford to run them, and even those who do get funding can rarely afford to pay a decent hourly rate. Being self-employed means not only no sick or holiday pay, but also no pay if the child is sick or if the family go on holiday, and you need to keep on top of the paperwork for the tax man. It can feel quite lonely if you only see your colleagues once a fortnight for a team meeting, and it takes a while to get to know people because you see them so infrequently. There can also be a lot of travel involved. Very few tutors are men, which is a shame as I think the children benefit from male role models, particularly as most of our children are boys. On balance I would recommend tutoring to bright, enthu-siastic people. Although at present the pay means it is difficult to make a long-term career out of in itself, especially outside London, it is a great way of getting experience in the fields of psychology and special education.

I hope my thoughts are of some interest to parents, educationalists or pro-spective tutors. I will shortly be leaving the area and so will no longer be working with Oli. I'd like to thank him and his family for being so good to work for, and wish them the best of luck for the future.

References

Buckman, S. (1995) 'Lovaas revisited: should we ever have left?' *Indiana Resource Centre for Autism Newsletter*, 8 (3), 1–7.

Burke, P. and Cigno, K. (2000) *Learning Disabilities in Children*. Oxford: Blackwell Science.

Jones, C. (2004) *Supporting Inclusive Education in the Early Years*. Buckingham: Open University Press.

Kolberg, K. (2004) 'Educational and biomedical interventions.' In T. Whitman (ed.) *The Development of Autism – A Self-Regulatory Perspective*. London: Jessica Kingsley Publishers.

Krantz, P., MacDuff, M. and McClannahan, L. (1993) 'Programming participation in family activities for children with autism: Parents' use of photographic activity schedules.' *Journal of Applied Behavioural Analysis*, 26, 89–97.

Leaf, R. and McEachin, J. (1999) *A Work in Progress: Behaviour Management Strategies and a Curriculum for Intensive Behavioural Treatment of Autism*. New York: DRL Books.

Lovaas, I. (1987) 'Behavioural treatment and normal educational and intellectual functioning in young autistic children.' *Journal of Consulting and Clinical Psychology*, 55, 3–9.

McBrien, J. and Felce, D. (1995) *Working with People who have Severe Learning Difficulty and Challenging Behaviour: A Practical Handbook on the Behavioural Approach*. Kidderminster: BILD Publications.

McConnell, M., Hilvitz, P. and Cox, C. (1998) 'Functional assessment: A systematic process for assessment and intervention in general and special education classrooms.' *Intervention in School and Clinic*, 34 (1), 10–20.

McCue, M. (2000) 'Behavioural interventions.' In B. Gates, J. Gear and J. Wray (eds) *Behavioural Distress: Concepts and Strategies*. London: Balliere Tindall.

Reed, J. and Head, D. (1993) 'The application of functional analysis in the treatment of challenging behaviour.' In I. Fleming and B. Stenfert-Kroese (eds) *People with Learning Disability and Severe Challenging Behaviour*. Manchester: Manchester University Press.

Smith Myles, B. and Southwick, J. (1999) *Asperger Syndrome and Difficult Moments*. Shawnee Mission, KS: Autism Asperger Publishing Co.

Thomas, G. and Vaughan, M. (2004) *Inclusive Education, Readings and Reflections*. Buckingham: Open University Press.

Chapter 7

John's Tale

Note: This final tale is somewhat different from the others as it is written by the person who undertook the learning, with a contribution from his sister. It is also different because John's programme started when he was 11 years old and, thus, it could hardly be categorised as 'early intervention'. However, as we used an ABA approach and many of the social programmes from the Lovaas curriculum, it is interesting for the reader to hear about John's learning. John is an extraordinary young person who has many talents. I thoroughly enjoyed working with him, his family and tutors and am delighted by his success.

My name is John and I have Asperger syndrome. This makes it difficult for me to explain how I feel about things, but it used to be even harder, until I found out about the condition and its effect on people like me. I guess I always did feel 'different' to my classmates – although 'mates' is probably the wrong expression, because they weren't really my mates at all. In fact, I'd heard the word but wasn't really sure what it meant. As for friends – well, what were they and how did you make them? I didn't know and it didn't really bother me that much because I felt happy enough by myself among my own things. I had my trains and my coin collection and as long as nobody messed them up, I was OK. I'm pretty fastidious like that. So, at primary school I was on the outside without knowing it and, now that I'm 16, I realise I wasn't very happy at all.

Looking back, there were some hurtful comments directed at me when I was at primary school. The girls tended to be worse than the boys. 'Oddball', 'weirdo' and 'queer' were quite common, but that might have had something to do with me wanting to stroke and smell their hair, which was (and still is) one of my little quirks, although I've just about got it under control now. I even remember my mother and father telling me about a parents' evening one time when a teacher, frustrated by the inconsistency of my class work, barked into my face, 'What's your problem, John?' As if I knew! At the time, though, the insults and name calling weren't so much upsetting as puzzling to me. Either way, I could have done without them, and it was a relief to get home so I could be around my own things again and not have to think about what was happening at school.

At about that time, my parents showed me an article in a national newspaper about something called Asperger syndrome. I didn't read it, but they explained about this boy who wanted *everything* done in a certain way and became aggressive if it wasn't. Apart from the last bit, they said I was very much like him. Obviously, this was a significant moment and things would never be the same again.

Mum started spending a lot of time on the telephone, and one evening, a few weeks later, I was introduced to a man my parents said would talk to me about my interests and how I was doing at school. He would write down what I said and I was to do my best. He was a clinical psychologist – whatever that was – and chatted to me about my coin collection, which I had taken along for him to see, and my trains. He was about to go to Canada so we talked about some of the great railway journeys of America. I never saw him again, but some time later, a report written by him about our conversation arrived and my parents said it showed I had Asperger syndrome. They seemed happy, so I was happy for them.

None of this made any difference at school. Sometimes my father had to escort me into class because the name calling in the playground was getting worse and, because I didn't understand, my parents thought it best to protect me from the more hurtful comments. There was talk about moving me to another school, but as I would soon be 12 and leaving anyway, nothing happened.

Again, Mum was on the phone a lot and said that we would be going to London soon to meet someone from an organisation which would be able to help me with my difficulties. This meant a long rail journey, so that was fine. Soon afterwards, I was told that Dr Anderson was coming all the way from London to see me. I didn't want her to come because I feel uncomfortable meeting new people, but at least I would get a trip to Leeds station out of it because she was arriving by train! When she got off, I didn't know what to do, so my parents shook hands with her while I jumped up and down and waved my arms around – another quirk which I've also learned to control.

Back home, Dr Anderson – or Maggie, as I was asked to call her – took me into the play room and we talked about my hobbies and how things were going at school. I said things were all right, although deep down I knew they weren't, and only looked at her when she wasn't looking at me. The following day she returned to London, which was OK by me, as it involved another exciting trip to the station to see her off. I think I gave her a hug this time!

For a while afterwards, the house seemed to be filled with strangers, coming one at a time, to be questioned by my parents, in the kitchen, away from me. It was explained to me that these would be the 'helpers' who would work with me on the programme Maggie had set up. In typical fashion, I suppose I felt a bit apprehensive, because these were people I didn't know, but my parents reassured me that they would only take on people I felt comfortable with and that I would have final approval. It was OK in the end, because the two students were easy to get on with – especially one called Katie, who was with me throughout the programme and is still a friend now.

So, for the next three years, two hours a night, three – sometimes four – times a week we worked through the programme. Katie with her tick sheets, me doing what I do – or used to do.

We started by constructing pictures of facial expressions and recognising feelings – non-verbal communication as it is called. I had to describe whether the face we had constructed showed a person who was happy or sad, angry or pleased, surprised, shocked, scared, worried and all points in between. Then – and this was the difficult bit – I had to copy the expressions myself in the mirror, being recorded on video all the while. The first session I spent with my head resting on the kitchen table – which may sound odd (it certainly looked it) – because I felt under a great deal of stress to 'perform' for the camera. Looking back at some of these films now, it is not me I'm watching, but someone else. Someone who waved his arms about, had peculiar facial tics, moved awkwardly and made no effort to communicate.

Of course, I didn't get it right at first. Some of the expressions I created for myself in the mirror looked like something out of Edvard Munch's *The Scream*! With time and practice, they began to look more natural, but it is always a shock when you first see yourself on camera. And there was a lot of practising to do, all of a sudden. In my bedroom, I acquired a full-length mirror to analyse posture and body language. Having rehearsed my moves in private, I then had to act these out in the garden for the camera, getting my arms to move in sync with my legs instead of leaving them hanging stiffly by my sides. Once I became more aware, the 'big arms' routine soon stopped.

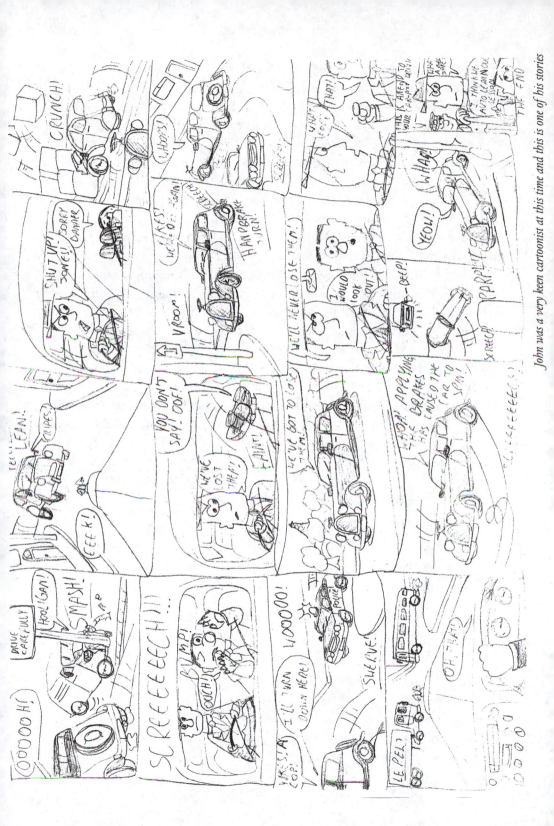

John was a very keen cartoonist at this time and this is one of his stories

One time, I was concentrating so hard, I lost my footing on the lawn and stumbled into a bush! Sometimes it was torture, especially having to watch the footage afterwards, but there were plenty of laughs too. Imagine watching *EastEnders* without sound. That's what I was required to do, all in the hope of recognising facial expressions – is that actor angry/sad/shocked/worried and so on? In *EastEnders*, there seemed to be a lot of angry people around.

We discussed why touching hair (and, by this time, noses) was unacceptable in public, so I soon learned to effectively become two people. There was the John who occasionally reverted to his old behaviour at home – and was tolerated – and there was the John who was on his best behaviour in the wider world, where 'lapses' were not allowed.

Then there was the verbal communication part of the programme. This consisted of holding conversations, using tone of voice and questions and statements. This was one of the most important – and possibly, for me, most difficult – parts of the programme as it showed me how to structure a conversation. But how do you start one in the first place? With Katie, I mostly had my head on the table and whenever she asked me a question I just grunted.

Looking back at the video it is hard for me to believe that I was once like this. I had no communication skills at all and I didn't know what to do if someone asked me a question. I just blushed with embarrassment and looked away. With a lot of practice, I grasped the idea of making an appropriate response and maintaining eye contact (without staring), so an example of a structured conversation, with Katie and I looking at each other across a table, might go something like this:

K: I like pizza – do you?
Me: Yes, I do. What other food do you like?
K: My favourite is a curry. What's yours?
Me: I don't like curry…

And so on.

Then it would become more complicated, with me having to start up a conversation:

Me: I don't like meat. I'm vegetarian.
K: Really? Why is that?
Me: I don't agree with killing animals for food.
K: How long have you been a vegetarian?
Me: Three years. Do you eat meat…?

And so on. And the video camera whirred, although by this time I had learned to ignore it.

Sometimes it was difficult to remember who was supposed to go next but at least it meant that I would be able to talk to people without them thinking I was odd. For instance, every Wednesday I could go into a paper shop to buy a copy of the *Beano*!

I also learned to use my voice with the right tone and volume, instead of mumbling or grunting. If we were in a car, I would have to use my 'loud' voice to make myself heard above the noise of the engine. I still don't like speaking loudly, although now I know I can if I have to.

Finally, there was the part of the programme dealing with emotions, trying to understand how people feel and why. Among the exercises was one where I had to write down what would make a certain person happy/sad/angry/afraid, so that I could empathise with him or her. There was also one where I had to imagine someone giving me a present, say a book, which I already had. I learned to say, 'Thank you', instead of, 'I've already got this', so that the person giving me the present wouldn't be hurt or upset. And there was one where I was asked how a person would feel if they really wanted something but were given a different present instead. Would they be happy or sad or would they try to make the best of it? This was hard work and I had to think very deeply about it. An example my parents use now is when my sister fell and hurt herself in the garden and I just stood and watched as she rolled around in pain. Now, if the same thing happened I would get help or try to find out what was wrong and if possible do something about it myself.

Maggie had been visiting us every few months to find out how the work was going, but the next time was a bit different because I was about to change schools. Wakefield Independent School was recommended by a tutor I was seeing privately for maths. After visiting the school, Maggie said it was just right for me because it was small (only just over a hundred pupils when I came) and the teachers were understanding and helpful. However, this would mean moving house, which was a bit upsetting for my younger sister Anna, who had made lots of friends.

This was a big event for us. We had never experienced moving house before and I remember the day we were moving. Everyone was rushing around, packing things in boxes; our close friends were helping; the removal people were putting chairs, tables and the piano in the van and we were told to sort our possessions into categorised boxes. It rained heavily all day and, although we liked our new house, it was in a terrible state when we first moved

A drawing John did around this time at school in response to the prompt: 'The old scarecrow appeared to dance in the eerie evening light and the taunting crows became an orchestra, conducted by his flailing arms'

in after years of neglect. I remember unloading only a few things and I just lay down on a mattress in the conservatory and there I fell into a deep sleep. It had been a very tiring day.

The good thing about the house was that it was only a few miles from our new school. The uniform was very smart and I looked forward to making a new start. But I was very nervous on the first day because I didn't know anyone and, although the teachers knew, none of my classmates had been told about my Asperger syndrome. After the way people had poked fun at me at the previous school, that was how I wanted it, but it meant I would have to apply what I had learned through the programme to avoid giving myself away. Four years later, no one has ever mentioned it, so I must be doing something right! I try to blend in, I have people I can call friends, and, while I still like my own company and a bit of peace and quiet, I know that I can hold conversations without getting too worked up about it. Sometimes I struggle, and I expect I always will in some situations, but nowhere near as much as before.

At home, I'm allowed to be more relaxed and can get away with doing things I know I must never do in the outside world, such as touching and smelling hair. So, some of the old behaviours are still there, but most are not. I haven't looked at my currency collection for years, but I've still got a thing about trains, so I joined a modelling club. I talk to the other members, help at exhibitions and look forward to going. Model cars are also a big interest and vie for space with a railway layout in my bedroom – but my latest hobby is playing the drums. Maybe that seems strange for someone who doesn't like loud noises, but I rehearse with two rock bands at school. Recently I played for the first time in public at speech night, which was a bit nerve-wracking, but I expect to be doing more soon. I would never have imagined having the confidence to do something like that before.

This is an important year for me. I am taking my GCSEs and people seem to think I should do well if I work hard and do my best. If all goes to plan I should be going to a sixth-form college we have found not far from the school I attend now. I am looking forward to that, but I am nervous too because my friends will be going to other colleges, so I will have to make new acquaintances. However, that is not as daunting a prospect as it was before. I don't know what will happen after that, but I hope to study law at university, preferably not too far away.

I try not to dwell on how I used to behave because they seem like the actions of a stranger – nothing to do with me! Like I said before, it is as if I was a different person then, one who had no kind of self-awareness. It was important for me to go through the programme, because otherwise I am sure I would have become increasingly unhappy, not understanding why people were poking fun at me, how to respond to them and what behaviours I would have to change to prevent it from happening. Now, I look forward to going to school because people accept me as I am, I like being with them and enjoy the routine. Sometimes I wonder what kind of state I would have been in without the intervention designed by Dr Anderson. But if I wonder too much I get upset.

A sister's perspective: a brother to me

Anna

I'm 12 now and think I was about eight years old when my parents told me that John was 'different' to other children and would need some sort of outside help. I can remember Mum explaining that there were certain foods it

A more recent pastel sketch by John

would be best for him to avoid eating, like bread and butter, as these contained gluten and dairy which might affect the way he behaved. It was all very complicated and I am still not sure I understand, but I remember once he was very ill after eating margarine when we were on holiday in Switzerland. We were halfway up a mountain and he had to lie down on a bench at the railway station. It sounds bad now, but at the time we found it funny and laughed at each other.

However, it brought home to me that John was not like most other people. Sometimes he could be a bit odd. One day, there seemed to be a trail of people coming to the house to interview John – or the other way round. They spoke to him about his interests and told him about theirs.

At the end of the day John had to choose who he wanted to work with on this programme which had been set up for him by Dr Anderson and I was told that I could join in with some parts of it too. Katie was the one John worked with most closely on the sessions which were held when we returned home from school. John would disappear into the kitchen and a few minutes later I would be called to join in with some of the fun, like games where we looked at cards with pictures of faces on them. John had to work out what their expressions meant and then imitate them, sometimes into a mirror or a video camera so he could see how he looked.

At school, John was getting bullied for stroking people's hair. He had always stroked mine so I didn't think anything about it, but it upset me that he was getting a hard time at school from people who didn't understand him. I told Mum and Dad what was going on at school, but it must have been difficult for John because although I had my friends he didn't seem to have any and was by himself all the time. Anyway, I was just as upset a few months later when it was announced that I would be leaving my friends behind because we were moving house to go to a different school – and even more upset when the house turned out to be a 300-year-old dump.

For a time, it was very disturbing to John's work. Everywhere seemed to be crumbling or falling apart or damp. Dad always seemed grumpy and there was a lot of talk about how much it would cost to repair our new home. I had been happy at the previous house and it was sometimes hard in our tatty new surroundings to understand why we had given all that up. It all seemed to be about what was good for John. But the sessions continued, and by this time they were being filmed on video, which we had fun with after John's programme had come to an end.

Later, we even made a film about ourselves in the form of a play where we acted out different roles. John was a guest on my TV show, playing a man called Hugh Effo who had been studying the meaning of life. We never got to find out what it was, though, because he kept trailing off. Another time, we created a film called *The Devil's Hotel* where I played the part of a half-man half-dog and John was a character called Ooman (human) who always got pushed around by the others. John would dress up in character and was responsible for most of the filming and direction. It was just a bit of fun and John seemed to enjoy himself.

So what is my brother like now? Well, he still has his annoying habits like touching my hair and calling me 'Baby Anna', which he knows winds me up. He is very good at drawing (which he always has been), he is obsessed with classic cars and trains – and he spends ages in front of the mirror every morning because he gets upset if his school tie is not straight. It drives me round the bend!!!! This is an example of a recent conversation, which took place at school. John comes up to me and points at his tie to ask if it is straight. Why doesn't he look in the mirror he always carries in his blazer pocket? But when I get angry I just pull it and he goes:

Him: No don't!
Me: Stop straightening it you berk. You're being paranoid about it!
Him: Well, I don't like it looking slack.

So he spends another half an hour in front of the mirror straightening it while pulling faces.

John has always liked classical music, but now he will listen to more modern stuff as well. Because he plays drums in two of the school bands all the boys in my class worship him, and say he is cool. At our previous school some people called him 'weirdo'. He has lots of friends, but he doesn't invite them to the house and they don't ask him to theirs. I play guitar, keyboards, flute and violin, so we sometimes play together. He usually drowns me out, but we have managed a few songs.

I can't tell you if he's changed much over the years because I'm too young to remember what he was like before. He takes things too seriously, but I now realise how difficult it has been for John and how much he has had to learn. Imagine not being able to recognise what someone feels by his or her facial expression or hold a conversation! No wonder he needed help.

As brothers go, he's OK.

Chapter 8

Moving Along

Autism and Rights

I have left this important area until the final chapter of this text for two reasons. The first is that this issue will, I feel, be at the forefront of the types of decisions we make about appropriate interventions for people with autism over the next ten years. The other reason is that I wanted it to come after the children's stories so that the reader can make his or her own judgement about the motivation and aims of the parents and professionals involved.

In this closing chapter, I would like to consider the movement that began in the US and Canada, of autistic adults who challenge discrimination and prejudice and promote the rights of people with autism. Those involved in this political and social movement clearly have many areas to address: however, we are concerned with one small but nevertheless significant area – that of the use of ABA as an educational tool for children on the autistic spectrum. The debate, which is beginning in the UK and has played a part in cases in the highest courts of law in Canada, is between adults with autism who eschew ABA intervention and parents (and professionals) who promote it. As the material in Chapter 2 intimated, this is a much bigger issue than the arguments that occur within the ABA community or between professionals advocating different types of early intervention. It concerns the entire concept of autism – how it is viewed philosophically, politically, socially and morally. The early intervention debate that is currently so hotly contested within the autism world has ramifications for the wider disability world, as the criterion of cognitive difference does not apply only to autism.

The debate is fierce: it concerns the hearts, minds and lives of the people engaged in it and their children. Much of the material is strongly written and emotive in character. However, I have tried to outline the issues as I perceive them and to comment upon them as a professional who uses ABA (amongst other approaches) to try to enhance the life opportunities for children on the autistic spectrum.

Autistic people or autistic behaviours?

This seems to me to be at the root of many of the disagreements between the two camps in this debate. Many autistic adults see autism as a defining aspect of themselves – that autism is as, or more, influential than gender or race in defining who they are (Sinclair 1993). Autism is not seen as a variant to their otherwise typical self, but as pervasive and essential. The position that is set up in opposition to this adopts the medical model – that autism is a condition/ disorder which afflicts the individual and that intervention can ameliorate it. Given that it is people's identity at issue here, there will be no easy resolution to this dilemma.

When we consider intervention for the child, if we take the former view of autism, addressing autism necessarily entails an attack on the individual's identity and, as such, is a violation of human rights. ABA intervention is described as 'program[s] designed not to educate but to transform that child into a different kind of child' (Dawson 2004). Lessons from other groups who trod the same political path that the autism groups are now beginning to follow indicate that this viewpoint is eminently sensible and equations of autism with gender (i.e. the way in which being a man/woman colours our relationship with ourselves and our world) make sense. However, the assumption that anyone who would suggest using particular teaching methods cannot, by definition, understand this stance is surely an overstatement of the case (Klein 2004). Many people, like me, who recognise the centrality of autism to individual's concept of self and relationship with the world, also feel that teaching can help the individual to gain skills and knowledge that will make life easier. More of this below.

Continuing our consideration of intervention from the 'autistic people'/ 'autistic behaviour' question, those espousing intervention are frequently parents of autistic children – autistic adults who have had or feel the need for intervention are not, as yet, particularly prominent in the discussions. Adults who are engaged in the 'autism advocacy' side of the debate have had suffi- cient education to enable them to engage: parents are just beginning the education path with their child. This is an unfortunate situation as emotions run considerably higher than if this were an adult–adult debate. However, the cartoon figure presented by the opponents of intervention is the parent who cannot accept the child's autism and who is using any tool he or she can to eradicate it. The parents' argument is that denial of the opportunity to undergo ABA is a denial of the child's right to an appropriate education.

Two very important things are occurring in the cartoon of parents who support ABA. The first is that parents are being accused of not loving their children – 'I am opposed to people who claim to love their child but not their autism' (Klein 2004). Michelle Dawson (2004) introduces the idea of false equations and false oppositions in her piece and this is a useful frame through which to view this particular issue. In my experience, and this is certainly true for the parents in this book, it is some aspects of a child's behaviour that parents wish to change, not the child.

The second thing that is happening is that the two groups are presented (mainly by each other) as having quite extreme views on the validity of any intervention at all and this is, again, a misleading caricature of the reality. Most parents using ABA are not 'at war' with autism – they are using what they perceive to be an effective teaching tool to help their children learn adaptive skills and behaviours. Similarly, the autism self-advocates are caricatured as promoting 'neglect' – leaving the child to develop without intervention. Again this is an overstatement of the case: what most autistic adults who are active in the field reject is the drive for 'indistinguishability' rather than the teaching of helpful skills (Schwarz 2004).

This leads us to the next area of debate in this consideration of people's rights in relation to intervention – that of how we decide what and how to teach.

Why teach? Teach what?

In the debate around whether we are trying to alter the nature of autistic children, a widely used analogy is that of being an elephant in an armadillo culture (e.g. Klein 2004). It is suggested that the very fact that elephants look like elephants, not armadillos, prevents us from trying to teach armadillo-like behaviour to an elephant. The argument then progresses to a situation in which the elephant did look like an armadillo and thus, all the other armadillos perceive his elephant-ness as problematic. This is a good analogy. However, at one point, the article (Klein 2004) states, 'and since this is an armadillo society, he must be trained to be an armadillo'. To link this analogy to the points made earlier about teaching, one might argue that while one would not seek to change the elephant into an armadillo, there may be some armadillo skills and knowledge that might be helpful to the elephant in living in an overwhelmingly armadillo culture. Herein lies the crux of the 'why teach/teach what?' issue: autistic people live in an overwhelmingly neuro-typical world.

I recall in the move to close institutions for people with learning disabilities in the 1970s, discussed in Chapter 2, there was much optimism about how, when people with disabilities were more 'seen' and became part of the community, prejudices would disappear and people's differences would magically no longer be problematic. Well, it's 30 years later and we're still working on it: people with learning disabilities face discrimination and prejudice on a daily basis. Thus, the autism advocates' plea for a more tolerant society is one which we must all not only endorse but work toward. In the mean time, we also need to equip people to live in the world we currently have. And for the child on the autistic spectrum, that means having a communication system, self-care skills, social skills and the chance to move through the education system. Some parents choose ABA as a means of reaching these goals.

A common theme in the literature emerging from the autism-advocacy field is rather a worrying echo of the paediatrician's 'wait and see' approach so many parents experience. Autism advocates suggest that parents are panicking and that their fears for their children's futures are unfounded.

> Parents of lower-functioning autistic children have to get used to the idea that…a lot of us were just as 'low functioning' in our childhoods as some of these people's children are now. (Klein 2004)

A little later in the same article (when discussing the strain on autistic people of acting non-autistic) the author writes, 'If you think that teaching people that they have to act like something they are not does not ruin them, you have not seen what I have seen.' I would like to balance this with a 'you have not seen…' of my own. A walk around a special needs school or a day centre for people with learning disabilities will reveal a great number of autistic adolescents and adults who have not gained skills, who have not grown into a 'self-sufficient, happy, capable autistic adult' (Klein 2004). Lack of appropriate teaching has left these adults with few skills, no opportunities for meaningful occupation or employment and little capacity for relationship building. Taking a chance that your child will be fortunate enough to grow into the ideal autistic adult is a chance not many parents would want to take.

The right to…

Thus, if parents wish to provide some help and support for their child, where do they turn? The political issues involved in this question have been raised in the text and I would like here to focus on why Lovaas intervention has gained such dominance in this question. I think that part of the answer is the whole 47 per cent issue. (For those unfamiliar with this, Dr Lovaas' original (1987) research claimed that 47 per cent of the children treated – 9 of 19 – were reported to have achieved normal functioning by the end of the intervention.) The implications of this statistic have, I feel, caused enormous difficulties for those parents and professionals who would like to work intensively with pre-schoolers, using an ABA approach. One of the major difficulties has been that 'recovery/indistinguishability' has become the criterion against which success is measured. Rather than considering the progress made by an individual child, the 'Is he in mainstream school? Does he have support?' questions spring to the fore. I would argue that this has done a huge disservice to both the integrity and utility of ABA. If we look back to consider Oli in Chapter 6 of this text, he is nowhere near 'normal functioning' but, of all the children in the text, has probably moved the furthest thus far in his life.

A more general point is that, in the literature, it often feels that Lovaas is the only option and that failure to undertake this intervention is to deny the child a basic human right. Indeed, this was the crux of the recent Auton case in Canada, which had and continues to have a deep and resonating effect on the way autism is viewed. To précis the course of the case: a group of parents in British Columbia (one of whose surname was Auton) began Lovaas intervention with their children. They requested that the government fund the programmes and recognise intensive behavioural intervention as a 'medically necessary service' (Carver 2001). When the government refused, the parents turned to law and, in 2000, the Supreme Court found in favour of the parents. The case then proceeded to appeal, the outcome of which was that while the children's programmes were funded, the intervention was not deemed 'medically necessary'. This outcome was hailed as a triumph by the autism rights movement – Michelle Dawson's response is entitled 'An Autistic Victory – The True Meaning of the Auton Decision' (Dawson undated). However, perusal of the Supreme Court of Canada decision (2004) shows that the basis of the decision did not lie with any issues of whether autism as a condition requires amelioration, but around Canadian citizens' right to 'core' and 'non-core' medical services. Thus, although not addressing the question directly, this case has added a further dimension to the 'right to intervention/right to no intervention' debate.

Consent

The final issue I wish to address from this emerging literature is the issue of consent as I feel that this area is destined to become a bloody battleground within the coming decade. Michelle Dawson writes, 'a project presuming to transform the nature of unconsenting clients through behaviour interventions must be challenged as to its ethics' (Dawson 2004). The parallel is drawn in her piece between Lovaas intervention for children on the autistic spectrum and the UCLA Feminine Boy Project, where feminine behaviours were replaced with masculine behaviours. (Again, we must recognise the historical context of the work: the condescension of history allows us all to be wise.) However, although we should not dispute the concept presented, we must ask whether most ABA practitioners and the parents who use it are, indeed, seeking to 'transform the nature' of their children. I would suggest not, but feel that this will not prevent an escalation of the debate.

Within the United Nations Convention on the Rights of the Child (UNICEF 1990), children are afforded rights based on two principles: what is in the child's best interests, and what is the age and maturity of the child concerned. If children are not considered to be competent to make decisions on their own behalf then their parents are thought to be the best people to make decisions for them. And, generally, parents do have their children's best interests at heart. However, I fear the difficulties ahead lie in the interpretation of that 'best interest'. Those battles will take place within a broader context of the changing ideological, political and social arena and we can but hope that those changes give us an alternative to a repeat of previous battles in the Lovaas/ABA field.

Summing up...moving on

Over the next decade, I am confident that much more will be learned about the causes of autism and the mechanisms involved in its presentation. I am also optimistic that the clarity this will bring will help to de-mystify the condition and thus debunk much of the dubious practice around care and intervention for children and adults with autistic spectrum disorder. I trust we can look forward to a time when each person receives appropriate teaching and support to live the life they choose and are, indeed, able to choose this support from a range of options.

However, having seen the pace of change in the learning disability field more generally, it is crucial that autism advocates do not try to walk this path alone. This group shares huge areas of political interest with other minority groups, particularly others with cognitive differences. It would be wasteful of talents, skills and time to fight this same battle separately. Second, there is, despite the impression given by some of the literature, a vast array of neurotypical people (parents, professionals in the field) who want to support the autistic person to be everything he or she wishes to be, including being autistic. In order to achieve real political change for people with autism, we need to move the debate away from infighting and toward the broader arena of ideological change, and this is something we can do together.

References

Carver, P. (2001) 'Disability and the allocation of health care resources: The case of Connor Auton.' *Health Ethics Today*, 12 (1). Available at www.phen.ab.ca/materials/het/het12–01b.html (accessed 8 December 2006).

Dawson, M. (2004) 'The Misbehaviour of Behaviourists: Ethical Challenges to the Autism-ABA Industry.' Available at www.sentex.net/~nexus23/naa_aba.html (accessed 8 December 2006).

Dawson, M. (undated) 'An Autistic Victory – The True Meaning of the Auton Decision.' Available at www.sentex.net/~nexus23/naa_vic.html (accessed 8 December 2006).

Klein, F. (2004) 'ABA Proponents Attack Autistics: Showing their True Character.' Available at http://home.att.net/~ascaris1/attacking-autistics.html (accessed 8 December 2006).

Lovaas, I. (1987) 'Behavioural treatment and normal educational and intellectual functioning in young autistic children.' *Journal of Consulting and Clinical Psychology*, 55, 3–9.

Schwarz, P. (2004) 'Another parent's take on ABA and its "defence".' Available at www.autistics.org/library/anotherparent.html (accessed 8 December 2006).

Sinclair, J. (1993) 'Don't mourn for us.' *Autism Network International*, 1, 3.

Supreme Court of Canada (2004) *Auton (Guardian ad litem of)* v. *British Columbia (Attorney General)* [2004] 3 S.C.R. 657, 2004 SCC 78. Available at http://scc.lexum.umontreal.ca/en/2004/2004scc78/2004scc78.html (accessed 8 December 2006).

UNICEF (1990) *Convention on the Rights of the Child*. Ankara: UNICEF.

Subject Index

Note: page numbers in bold refer to illustrations.

Author Index

DATE DUE

FEB 18 '09			